DEAN MANNIX

PROTECT AND PROVIDE

CUSTOMER-CENTRIC (AND COMPLIANT) INSURANCE SALES

#1 INTERNATIONAL BEST-SELLING AUTHOR

WEBSITE: www.deanmannix.com

LINKEDIN: linkedin.com/in/deanmannix

AUTHOR WEBSITE: www.deanmannix.com

EMAIL: dean@salesitv.com

1st Edition 2017

First Published 2017 for Dean Mannix by Evolve Global Publishing

PO Box 327 Stanhope Gardens NSW 2768 info@evolveglobalpublishing.com

www.evolveglobalpublishing.com

BOOK TYPOGRAPHY: RJ2

ISBN: (Paperback) 978-0-6480606-0-4

ISBN: (Hardcover) 978-0-6480606-2-8

ISBN(Createspace) 978-0-6480606-3-5

ISBN: (Smashwords) 978-0-6480606-1-1

ASIN: (Amazon Kindle) B072PTQKP3

This book is available on Kobo and Apple iBooks (digital)

TABLE OF CONTENTS

For my two "Dads".

My father Kevin and mentor Brian.

Both of you passed away too soon.

PREFACE

If you sell insurance, you're a hero.

That may sound like an overstatement, but until you've been through an insurance event (with or without insurance), you simply cannot understand the impact insurance has on the lives of the people impacted by the unexpected.

And without insurance salespeople, that impact would almost always be life destroying.

I've written this book because, at the age of 15, my life and the lives of those I love were impacted by the very unexpected murder of my father. I've written this book because while all the money in the world couldn't replace the love I have for my father; a lack of insurance made it significantly more difficult to deal with the aftermath.

Before you start feeling sorry for me, let me explain something only people that have lost a parent at a young age can understand. It really doesn't matter how the parent died. What matters is the impact losing that parent has on your life and the lives of the people you care about. You and your family are the ones left behind.

The loss of my father didn't kill me. It made me stronger, and it made me care about others. It taught me the importance and value of managing the risk in your life, where that risk has the potential to impact others you love. It taught me that the unexpected does happen; even to those you think are invincible. It taught me the value and importance of insurance.

But it also taught me that many people selling insurance are often unconsciously behaving like villains.

Failing to help customers understand the real consequences of an insurance event and the risk they should consider covering is not heroic. Selling insurance more focused on the person's budget than on the risk their personal situation creates is not heroic behaviour. Deliberately avoiding discussions about a person's personal situation to avoid any risk of giving advice is not heroic. Promoting this sort of behaviour as part of a compliance strategy is arguably evil. Backing down, when potential customers default to objections based on ignorance and short-term thinking, is not the behaviour of a hero. Blaming this sort of behaviour on the need to make budget, is not heroic. And claiming that you can only sell this way, because of the challenging compliance environment or an inability to provide personal advice, is the behaviour of someone that lacks the courage a truly customer-centric insurance salesperson needs.

This book is about developing your courage and your power in insurance sales situations. It's about selling compliantly and selling successfully. If you're truly customer centric, there shouldn't be a need to balance these two demands of the profession. Compliance will flow if your mindset is truly customer centric, and you're skilled in educating and ethically motivating better customer decisions. If you're not licensed to offer advice, don't let that be an excuse for selling the insurance people want to pay for instead of selling them the insurance they need. I'll show you how to achieve a truly customer-centric result without making recommendations.

This book is about providing you with a strategy and set of skills that will enable you to be the hero you need to be. It's about showing you how to sell insurance in a manner that's truly customer centric.

What you do is heroic, and I thank you for all the people that are insured because you have the courage to sell insurance.

INTRODUCTION

For the past 20 years, I've done nothing but think, and get paid to think, about how to sell more effectively and efficiently. I'm blessed that this has enabled me to work with many of the best companies in the world across more than 25 countries. This has included literally thousands of hours of consulting, coaching, training and conference speaking for insurance companies and their people. I've also reviewed and provided advice and feedback on over 2500 insurance sales phone calls.

My goal in this book is to develop you as a professional.

In this book, I'm going to focus solely on the direct practical applications of the strategies and thoughts I share to selling life insurance. No matter what type of insurance you sell, every strategy I provide will be relevant and useable in your common insurance conversations and selling situations. I'm going to focus on life insurance because this is the insurance most valuable to families and the loved ones of those who suffer an insurance event. It's arguably also the most difficult type of insurance to sell.

For most of this book, I'm going to speak to you directly as the insurance salesperson, because that's where the sales happen. At times, I'll provide commentary aimed at leaders within the business because the environment they create for you will have a dramatic impact on your ability to perform. If you're a sales manager, understand that taking the salesperson's perspective is the key to great coaching and leadership. This book will enable you to coach performance and compliance in the same conversation. If you're the CEO, understand that your culture is the sum of how your salespeople and those supporting them feel, engage and behave. If nobody sells insurance, you don't have a business. This book will challenge you to make your salespeople and the way they engage customers your number one priority.

When I say,

"sales"

I have little doubt someone in compliance has just red-flagged this book. And that's part of the challenge the insurance industry must tackle head on.

Insurance needs to be "sold" if society is ever going to conquer the underinsurance issue.

And because insurance needs to be "sold" I'm going to call anyone that sells insurance an insurance salesperson. Many of you will find that label disturbing. I know that many of you will be saying,

"But Dean, I'm an advisor or a relationship specialist or some other title. I'm NOT an insurance salesperson."

And that's your biggest problem.

Until you can acknowledge that the core of your role is to sell, you will never achieve excellence in sales. And failure to achieve excellence in your sales skills, behaviours and beliefs will not only impact your earnings, it will make it more likely that the people you engage with will leave the insurance conversation underinsured and ignorant about the real risk they're taking with the wellbeing of those they love.

A huge part of the problem here is that insurance companies are trying to distance themselves from the word "sales". There's a false belief that changing the words they use to describe what must happen and what their front-line people must be, will protect their brand and deliver better experiences for their customers. This is simply not the case. In fact, it's the opposite.

As a formerly practising lawyer, I understand the challenges compliance teams face in ensuring a compliant environment. I understand insurance companies must protect their brand as the source of confidence in those they insure. Having said that, I'm consistently disappointed that customer centricity and customer experience suffer so dramatically at the hands of compliance and legal teams. This is rarely a consequence of deliberate and conscious thought. It's a consequence of fearing a non-compliant sale more than fearing no sale at all.

And here's the problem I have with that attitude. It results in literally tens of thousands of people remaining underinsured and ignorant of their real insurance needs. It results in millions of dollars of premiums forgone that could have been sold in an entirely compliant manner. And it limits the capability and destroys the confidence of frontline salespeople tasked with achieving sales.

Leaders need to vision sales and service cultures that enable and drive a customer-centric approach to selling that delivers great sales results AND perfect compliance. Improved sales skills, coaching and confidence, can and does support significantly higher levels of compliant customer engagement. It is the person without sales skills that is more likely to cut corners to achieve a sale in a non-compliant manner. It's also the salesperson without sales skills that is more likely to achieve a sale that is compliant but fails to truly cover the customer's real risk.

I repeat – insurance must be sold.

It's not natural for humans to take pain today to avoid an uncertain negative event that may or may not occur tomorrow (or later today). It's also generally the people and families with the tightest budgets that suffer the most when an insurance event occurs. And experience from listening to literally thousands of calls tells me most people overestimate the sufficiency of cover provided by employment-based insurance schemes (like superannuation and group plans).

As a society, we should and must be concerned about these three causes of underinsurance and avoidance of the insurance conversation.

As an insurance salesperson, the core of your role is to equip yourself with the skills required to move people through these three excuses. Your skills and confidence determine how many of the people you talk to are enabled to make conscious, informed and deliberate decisions about the wellbeing of those they love.

Please note that I didn't say,

"Your skills and confidence determine how many people you sell insurance to."

That's not what this book is about. The customer-centric way of sales is about helping people buy and in that context, let's consider your role as an insurance salesperson.

Your role includes engaging as many people as you can in insurance conversations. If you're not genuinely passionate about making sure every person you speak to understands their risk situation you're not truly customer centric. Customer centricity includes genuinely caring about the wellbeing of the people you engage.

Your role in the insurance conversation includes helping people understand the risk their families and loved ones face if an insurance event occurs. This includes educating people on how to determine how much downside they and their families face. Truly customer-centric insurance conversations also help people quantify the consequences of a lack of cover should an insurance event occur.

As challenging as it is, your role also includes helping people understand what risk they're able to cover with the insurance provider(s) you access or with whom you work.

Where their health or other conditions limit their ability to access insurance your role is to let them know what they can cover.

I refer to this as "the work".

The insurance salesperson willing to do the work will sell more, enjoy customer relationships more, get referred more and sleep better at night. If you're willing to do the work and develop the skills required to sell/close in a customer-centric manner, the insurance industry will provide you with a highly fulfilling career.

Having done the work, you have a right to ask them to decide on how much of that risk they're willing to pay to cover. Notice I call this a "right" rather than referring to it as a sales strategy or part of your role.

The distinction is that if you've done the work you have the right to close. Not to close the sale but instead the right to close the decision. Whether you're able to provide personal advice or not, an important part of your role is to encourage people to make an informed decision on how much uncovered risk they are willing to tolerate.

If you've helped someone understand and quantify their insurance needs and options, failing to ask for a decision is choosing to leave them in an uninsured state. People need help to make the right decisions for themselves and their families. And salespeople that have done the work have no need to fear people making those decisions one way or another.

I can appreciate many of you can't provide advice and recommendations on how much or what insurance people should put in place. Despite this, all of you can and should be able to deliver on this job description in a completely compliant manner.

This is the customer-centric way.

If it sounds and looks like hard work, you may need to consider another role. The more you care for the wellbeing of the people you speak to, the less this feels like work. And the more you do the work at the front end of the conversation the more likely it is people will choose to cover all or part of the risk in their lives. Importantly, the more likely it is they'll choose to do that with you.

In this book, I'll share customer-centric skills, attitudes and strategies that have been proven by many of the best companies and insurance salespeople in the world. If you're committed to becoming part of that club, I'm committed to helping you.

First, you need to develop a truly customer-centric mindset. I call this the protect and provide mindset. The more you develop a belief in the need for insurance, confidence in engaging in insurance conversations and resilience to failure and indecision, the more you're going to enjoy your profession.

Mental preparation is critical but so is efficiency and effectiveness.

A defined process for taking the customer through their insurance purchasing journey is going to enable you to do the right things at the right time. I'll introduce you to the ROI Sales Methodology, and this will enable you to chunk down all the skills you need to develop. Chunking the conversation into smaller bite-size skill sets will enable you to consistently reflect on and improve each skill, capture proven practice and repeat it. The more you analyse, understand and repeat the strategies that make you successful, the easier the work becomes.

Before we "deep dive" in to how to achieve excellence in each step of the ROI Sales Methodology we'll consider things from the customer's perspective. I'll introduce you to the PAVE Principle. We'll deep dive in to the psychology behind why people avoid the insurance conversation and how to generate the perception that there is both a problem to be solved and value to be expected. This understanding will significantly shift the way you're approaching sales and enable you to engage in truly customer-centric conversations that also deliver sales results.

Sales process and methodology matters but it's not very useful if nobody will engage with you in an insurance conversation. Turning a lead into a conversation is a critical and poorly understood skill across most of the insurance industry.

Doing the numbers and sacrificing countless leads is not heroic behaviour. And the downside is not just all the people that remain underinsured despite your call. There's a significant cost to your business and brand. I'll provide you with proven strategies for significantly improving your conversion of leads to insurance conversations.

To be successful, you'll need the skills required to engage in insurance conversations that create amazing customer experiences and motivated insurance purchasers. We'll go through each element of the ROI Sales Methodology and share best-practice strategies for increasing the likelihood that people will want to explore their needs and risks with you. I'll explain how to shift from selling insurance to helping people buy insurance at each step of the journey.

As part of that journey we need to ensure you're rewarded for your hard work. You need to have the skills to turn conversations into decisions. We'll discuss how to close in a customer-centric manner that is both compliant and ethically persuasive. If you've done the work, this should be the easiest part of the conversation.

We'll discuss objections and how to handle them but the customer-centric way is all about avoiding objections and only selling to people with real needs that are ready to buy.

If people are genuinely covering all the risk they and their families face, this is likely to be a big decision. If people aren't a little challenged by the amount of premium they need to pay to cover the risks they genuinely face, then there's a good chance you've been more focused on selling to affordable premiums rather than real needs. Some insurance is better than none, but the right amount of cover should always be your goal. This means you're going to need strategies for giving people time to think and engage others in the decision. I'll share how the best do this and increase their conversion rates through a multi-contact strategy.

Remember – easy and fast sales generally result in fast and difficult cancellations.

Once again, if this all seems too hard, then I suggest another career. The day of the quick sale and self-centred insurance salesperson is coming to an end. I'm excited about that because that's the first step in transforming the industry into a credible profession that people see and experience as being valuable and customer centric.

If you're up for the work, I promise you this book will take you on a journey that guarantees success for you, your company and, most importantly, your customers.

LEGAL WAIVER

Unfortunately, I can't guarantee that everything you'll read in this book will be completely aligned to the opinions and interpretations of your compliance team. Because of that, I need to stress that nothing in this book should be considered legal advice.

Please consult your compliance team for guidance if you have any doubt as to whether a strategy suggested in this book is appropriate for your sales situations.

Always remember that the core of your compliance team's purpose is to protect the customer, the company that pays your wages, the brand that pays claims, and your career. Compliance teams are generally doing the best that they can. They don't wake up each morning wondering how they can make it harder to make sales and more difficult to deliver amazing customer experiences.

Having said that, one of the biggest challenges salespeople and CEOs will face in our industry is unchallenged compliance processes and policies that put a fear of noncompliance ahead of the needs and interests of customers. Unfortunately, the discretionary nature of many of the laws that govern the insurance industry make this more likely than not.

If your compliance team has a challenge with anything I share in this book I would love to hear from you. As an industry, those that sell insurance must get on the front foot and be courageous in ensuring the way you sell truly helps customers make better decisions about insuring their risks.

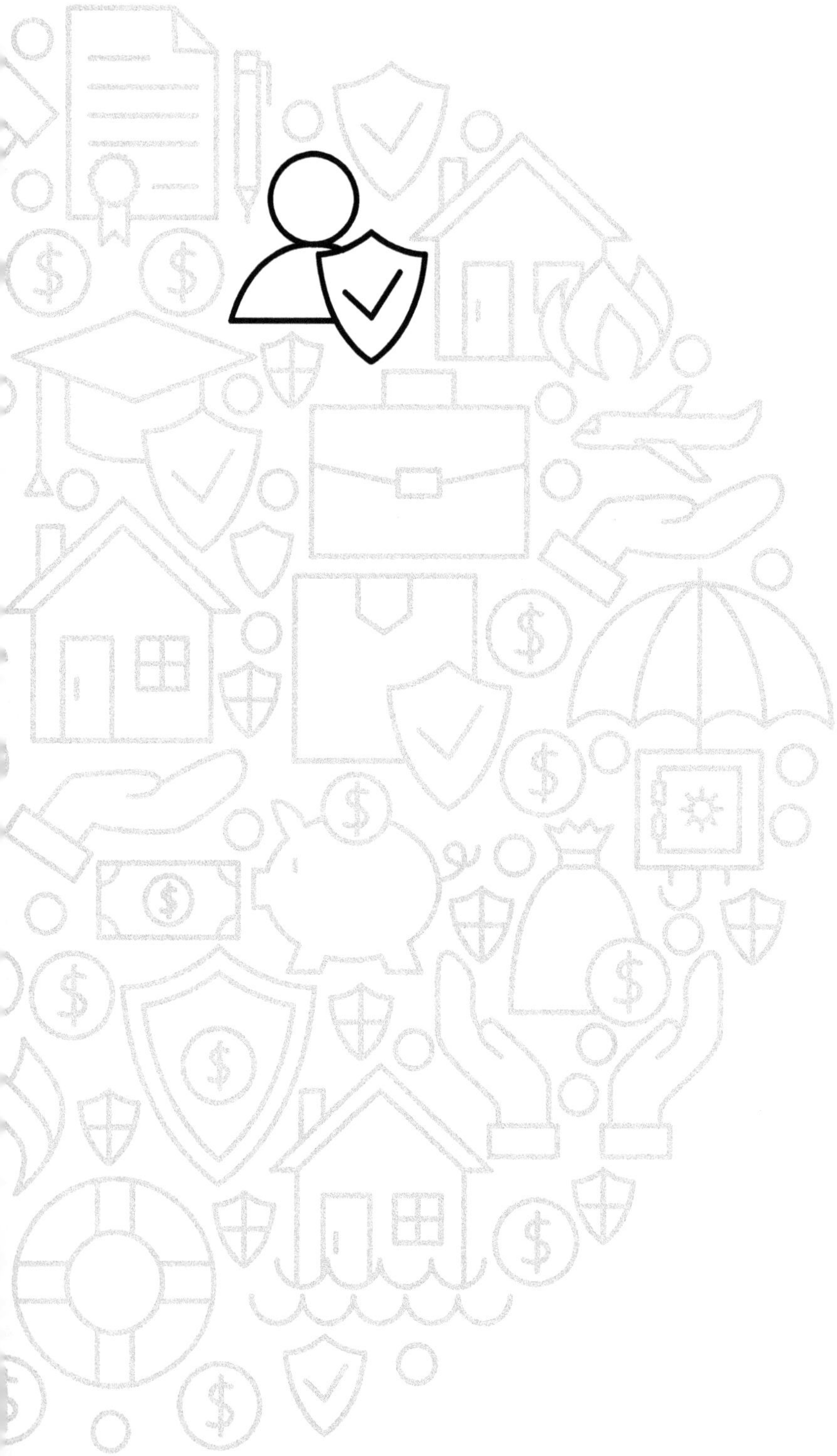

CHAPTER ONE

THE PROTECT AND PROVIDE MINDSET

THE CHALLENGES WE ALL FACE

No matter how good you are as an insurance salesperson, there are several challenges you face in being effective and efficient in your role.

First, we must deal with the natural aversion to the insurance conversation. People unconsciously avoid this discussion, and I'll explain why that is in the next chapter. This makes it hard because it means you need to be excellent at engaging people that don't necessarily want to discuss insurance despite needing insurance.

Second, we're dealing with humans full of biases that cause them to make poor decisions around what's important when buying insurance. Even if you're speaking to someone that's motivated to buy insurance, there's a high probability they're underestimating how much they'll truly need to provide for themselves and their families if an insurance event occurs. There's also a high probability they're more focused on what they'll have to pay in premiums than they are on the quality of cover they're buying.

Third, we're dealing in a highly regulated market, passing laws that seem to assume you'll be dishonest. The amount of disclosure and compliance-related paperwork required is increasing significantly, and the laws tend to assume you were in the wrong, unless you can absolutely prove you were in the right. That makes it hard because you're being challenged to have a very personal conversation in a legally compliant manner.

Fourth, more than ever, companies need to protect their brand, and their ability to maintain the necessary regulatory approvals to sell insurance and other financial products. So, decisions get made that are significantly more focused on ensuring compliance than customer experience. When the compliance teams are writing the sales scripts, we know there's a very high likelihood that it will be difficult for you to engage in a customer-centric manner.

Fifth, the response to many of these challenges has been to operate on a limited or general advice basis. If you're in this space, you know how challenging it can be to sell to someone that's asking you for advice that you can't give.

Finally, all of this is leading to decisions being made too far away from the insurance conversation. Leaders are far too fixated on generating more leads, being price competitive, converting as many leads as possible as fast as possible and maintaining 100% compliance. This fixation causes a lack of focus on the customer experience, the ability of their people to engage in a personal, needs-based manner, the importance of educating customers and selling over multiple calls to improve customer experience and the fit of insurance they purchase.

The reason most insurance conversations are not truly customer centric is not that insurance salespeople don't want to be customer centric. Company-focused compliance strategies, a lack of customer-centric sales skills, poor compliance-focused sales coaching, beliefs driven by too much focus on price, quality assurance processes that fail to truly consider customer experience and a host of other factors are to blame.

So, what's the answer? How do we overcome these challenges?

There's no easy answer, but I suggest the way forward is linked to a combination of the "front-page test" and the "happy employee" test.

I was lucky enough to consult to Macquarie Bank globally throughout the 2000s. As they became one of the most profitable investment banks in the world, CEO Allan Moss was arguably more committed to maintaining a compliant and risk focused culture than he was on driving a sales and profit focused culture.

He knew he couldn't be everywhere around the world as they expanded. He also knew he was hiring very smart leaders and people that were committed to turning their ideas and hard work into profit for the bank and bonuses for themselves. To balance up the requirement to manage risk and the need to reward people for profitable behaviours, his solution was to put in place a very simple but powerful test. The test was called the front-page test, and it asked people to consider the following question before taking any action.

"Would you do it or say it if you knew it was going to be on the front page of the newspaper tomorrow?"

No matter where you worked in the business this test made it very clear what behaviour was not appropriate. It reminded everyone within the bank that ethics mattered and profit would never be accepted as a trade-off.

In the insurance space, I think companies need to go one better. There needs to be a recognition that ethics and compliance are only one part of the complex insurance puzzle.

If we borrow from Sir Richard Branson, a core mantra within the Virgin group of companies is:

"Clients do not come first. Employees come first. If you take care of your employees, they will take care of the clients."

If you're the CEO of an insurance company, how convinced are you that your frontline insurance salespeople are happy enough in their roles to make your customers happy? What do you think it would take to make them truly happy in their roles?

My point here is that an employee that is disempowered by a lack of skills and coaching and/or company-focused compliance measures, is unlikely to truly engage the customer in a customer-centric manner. I'm sure many compliance people are saying to themselves,

"Yeah but Branson is loose, and he runs high-risk companies by the seat of his pants."

But – that would be ignoring the fact that the airlines he runs operate in arguably the world's most compliant environment. It would also ignore that Virgin has found a way to enable its cabin crew to deliver compliance announcements in a fun, customer-centric manner that provides for both the customers' safety and the crew's need to enjoy their role.

So, in the insurance space, we need to ensure that we adopt and employ a guiding test that meets the needs of the company, the needs of the customers and the needs of the people selling insurance.

THE PROTECT AND PROVIDE TEST

I propose the following test for everyone within the insurance industry when considering anything that impacts customer experience. Before you decide on how you will respond or act in any situation simply consider this:

Will it?

1. Protect the customer from their real risks and provide adequate cover for them and their loved ones

AND

2. Protect the company's brand and provide adequate profit for the risks taken

AND

3. Protect our people's careers and their ability to sell within the industry

AND

4. Provide enough flexibility to engage customers in a truly customer centric manner

AND

5. Enable our people to financially provide fairly for themselves given the difficulty and risk involved in selling insurance

You'll notice the "AND" throughout the test. Gail Kelly, the former CEO of Westpac, one of the largest banks in the world, was famous for demanding the "AND". She was constantly demanding sales results AND great service AND higher productivity. As challenging as this was for the Senior Executives I've worked with,

DEAN MANNIX | PROTECT AND PROVIDE

it was a powerful way to drive home the importance of developing strategies and systems to enable front-line people to balance potentially conflicting demands AND still achieve amazing results.

Let's apply the test to several common insurance situations to explain how the test highlights the need for change.

Mark is a customer-centric advisor taking care of Paul's wealth advice and financial planning. Paul is 45 years old and owns his terrace in a great suburb in Sydney. He's single with no dependants and has a superannuation policy that provides income protection and life insurance. Mark prides himself on not selling to his clients and only discussing insurance where there's a clear need. He makes the decision not to discuss life insurance with Paul because he doesn't think there's a need.

I have no doubt Mark really believes he's being customer centric by not selling insurance to Paul. But he's completely forgotten that protecting Paul means he needs to make sure Paul's loved ones are protected and can provide for Paul if an insurance event happens. Mark forgot that people often don't die from horrific accidents and need to be cared for by their families. This is a true story, and Paul also thought he had no need for insurance until another advisor asked a simple but powerful question.

"What if something happened to you and your parents had to look after you for the rest of your life?"

His terrace would have been completely unsuitable to house an incapacitated person. His parents weren't wealthy enough to pay for all the services Paul would require if he was incapacitated and their lives would have been turned upside down if they had to become his primary carers. The burden of this is the last thing he would have wanted to emotionally deal with if he ended up in a state where he required full-time care. And when he did the sums, the financial impact on his loved ones would have been dramatic despite the equity he had built up in his home.

The customer-centric insurance professional realises that protecting loved ones is part of their role as a professional insurance salesperson.

And they realise that making assumptions about the customer's situation, and decisions for the customer based on those assumptions, is not customer centric.

This behaviour failed to provide for the wellbeing of Paul's loved ones, so it failed our protect and provide test.

John is one of the highest performing salespeople at All About the Bucks Insurance. He has one of the highest conversion rates in the team and consistently gets customers across the line that didn't think they needed insurance until he sold them on the importance of having cover. His killer strategy is asking people how much they think they could afford per week and building cover around that amount. Compliance is happy with this as they're concerned about laws protecting low-income earners and the need to prove affordability.

I have no doubt John is considered a star within his business. And I have no doubt people are justifying his behaviour by saying something like,

"At least those people have some insurance in place, and they can afford what's been sold to them."

But this is NOT customer centric. The reason it's not customer centric is that the sale is based on the customer's budget rather than the risk they need to cover. The person that's purchased insurance is probably feeling great because they think buying insurance has protected them from an insurance event and will provide for their family if that involves death or total and permanent disability. But we know that's not likely to be the case if the insurance conversation focused on the budget they wanted to allocate rather than the risk they and their family are exposed to.

John's budget-focused strategy is not truly protecting customers from the risks they face or providing adequate cover, so it fails our protect and provide test.

Mary is considered an excellent quality assurance expert in her business. She's pushed incredibly hard to make sure privacy laws are strictly adhered to, and people know that if they fail to ask the three key identification questions early in the call, they'll be punished in their QA scores. She lobbied management to make sure this would impact salespeople's commissions, and compliance breaches relating to privacy breaches are at an all-time low on inbound calls. She's even made sure team leaders in the call centre know that they need to coach the use of identification questions at the start of calls.

I have no doubt Mary is considered highly by management, and I acknowledge a decrease in non-compliant calls is critically important within any insurance business. But here's the problem. The need for compliance is the company's need rather than the customer's need. The customer didn't call in expecting the first part of the engagement to be all about the company meeting its compliance needs. I'm not suggesting identification questions shouldn't be asked. But I do know from consulting on thousands of calls that an aggressive focus on compliance behaviours early in an inbound call breaks rapport with the customer, makes it more difficult for the insurance professional to engage them in a rapport-building conversation and often causes customers to have to go through an identification process twice when they must be transferred to another person. If the company were committed to customer centricity, they would educate their people to engage inbound callers on a personal level, ascertain what they needed help with and then ask identification questions once they confirmed they could help.

The customer-centric organisation recognises that its compliance strategies must provide for the customer's needs AND protect the company. High compliance rates do not necessarily correlate to high customer satisfaction.

Mary's succeeding in protecting the company's brand. But her lack of focus on the quality of the customer's experience makes it difficult for the insurance professionals working in the business to be successful in meeting customer needs and in achieving high conversation to customer conversion rates. So, it fails our protect and provide test.

James is a highly motivated trainer and coach within All About the Bucks Insurance – a company that loves sales training. Conversion rates on the leads provided have been dropping off, and he's been asked by the General Manager to run several objection handling and closing clinics across the team to get the numbers back up. James runs the sessions providing a host of great examples and role plays of how to use closes throughout the call and how to deal with common objections. Following the training, there's an immediate improvement in conversion.

I'm sure many reading this would think James is awesome and needs to be recognised. If you're in marketing, you're happy because lead conversion is improving and your cost per customer is dropping. If you're the salesperson, you're happy because you're earning more commission and that probably means your leader is getting paid more as well. And if you're the General Manager you're happy because profits should be rising.

But here's the problem. Did anyone ask themselves why the team was getting so many objections in the first place? Did anyone consider that more sales driven purely through objection handling and closing are generally linked to a lack of customer centricity in the sales process? Has anyone considered this from the customer's perspective?

I can't be certain here, but I'm confident that an analysis of the calls would show that the way people are selling is not truly protecting and providing for the customers. It is highly likely that this approach fails our protect and provide test.

Betty is a top performer in the sales team who's known for first call closing. She's fantastic at getting customers to make quick decisions through a combination of closing, focusing customers on how small premiums are compared to cover and handling common objections. She also has a fantastic average call handling time because she avoids getting into too much detail about the customer's situation to make sure she avoids giving any advice in the call. This enables her to maintain great quality assurance scores because everything she does is compliant. All of this is leading to getting paid extremely well despite the fact the policies she sells have a higher than average cancellation rate in the first 12 months of purchase.

Until the last point, many people were probably thinking,

"I wish I were Betty"

or

"I wish we could hire more Betty's"

This is a fail on all the first four aspects of the test and arguably the fifth.

1. The way Betty sells reduces the likelihood the customer will be protected from their real risks or that adequate cover will be purchased to provide for them and their loved ones.

2. When people cancel policies (or try to cancel), there's brand damage.

3. Betty is compliant but the way she sells is not truly meeting customer needs, and her success is likely to be negatively impacted as legislation makes that a genuine priority.

4. Betty is held up as a hero for selling quickly and on the first call, and this is subconsciously promoting a lack of customer centricity in her sales process.

5. Betty is arguably getting paid more than "fairly" because there are no consequences for cancellations above the average.

I hope these examples give you an understanding of how you could be using the protect and provide test both personally and within your organisation.

Organisations need to understand that measures put in place to protect the company often lead to a failure to protect and provide for both the customer and the person selling the insurance. Companies truly committed to customer centricity understand that every aspect of the business needs to achieve all five aspects of the test. At the very least, all five aspects should be considered and discussed when considering new and existing systems and initiatives within the business.

Some of you may be asking yourselves,

"How do I apply this personally?"

The bottom line is that you need to stop doing anything that doesn't protect and provide for the customer AND protect and provide for the company you work for AND protect and provide for you and those you love.

As an insurance professional, you can only control what you can control, and that's where your focus needs to be. But no matter how challenging the environment in which you sell, you can absolutely control the following:

- Your ability to engage a customer in an insurance conversation that educates you and the customer on the risks they face and the amount of cover they truly need to provide for themselves and those they love.

- Your commitment to selling in a manner that protects customers and their loved ones from those risks.

- Your commitment to developing your skills around successfully selling in a compliant manner to protect both your career and the brand of the insurer behind the cover you sell.

- Your commitment to working as hard and as smart as you must to make sure your results enable you to provide for yourself and your family.

If you're willing to make those commitments and take the action that flows from them, I can promise you a long, rewarding and fulfilling career within the insurance industry.

In the Appendix, I've shared the Protect and Provide Code. This is a tool you can download at **www.deanmannix.com** so you can put it on the wall, read it daily and over time build your commitment and ability to truly live this as part of the way you sell insurance.

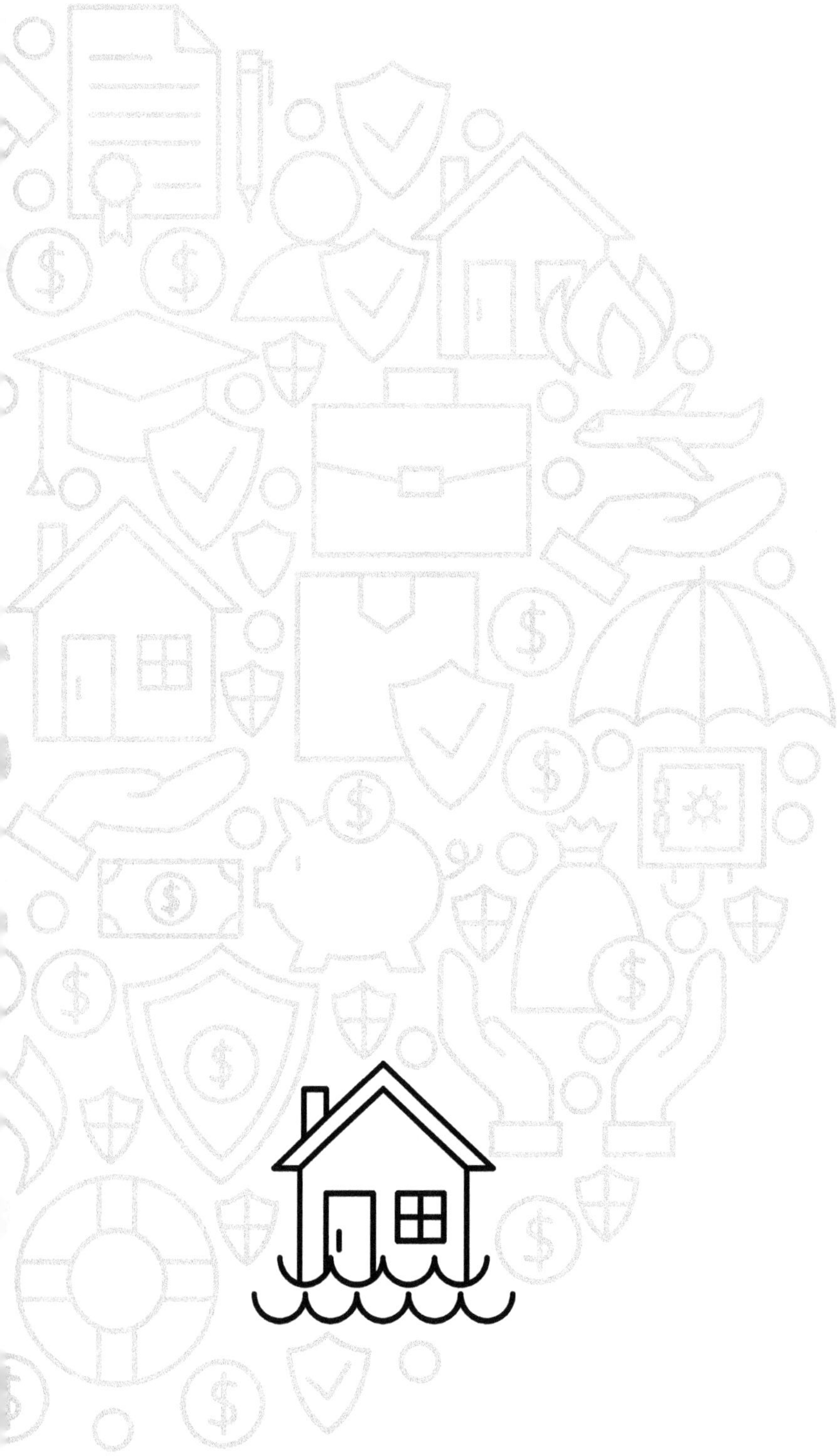

CHAPTER TWO

Selling Problems and Value vs. Products, Pricing and Benefits

WHAT PROBLEMS DO YOU SOLVE?

I want to put a challenge to you before you read this chapter.

I want you to write down all the problems you solve for the customers you sell insurance to. No matter what type of insurance you sell, take a little time out before you read ahead and write down as many as you can.

Please do this exercise before you read on. Spend at least 5 minutes on it. As an example, if you sell life insurance I can give you more than 10 important problems that having adequate cover in place can solve for a customer.

The more you understand the problems you solve with the insurance you sell, the easier selling becomes. And the more the customer perceives your insurance is solving a problem, the more valuable they perceive your insurance solution is. I'll come back to this in later chapters, but before we move ahead, let's consider why I want you to focus on problems rather than benefits.

PROBLEMS OR BENEFITS?

For this chapter, don't be concerned about the compliance challenges you may have with making statement B if you're only able to provide general advice. I won't be encouraging you to make statements that are this aggressive. In fact, I won't be encouraging you to make statements at all. I simply want to use this comparison to share some very important psychological findings of what motivates customer behaviour. Customer behaviour includes the way customers engage, share information, and make decisions (including the decision to procrastinate).

There are two statements below. I want you to consider which statement you think is more likely to result in a person choosing to take cover? Ideally, take a little time out to write down why you think that. Another thing I want you to do before reading on is to quantify how much more successful the statement chosen would be compared to the other statement.

STATEMENT A.

We can insure you for $400,000 of cover for $76 per month. If something happens to you and you take this insurance your family will receive a payout of $400,000.

STATEMENT B.

S tatement B. We can insure you for $400,000 of cover for $76 per month. From what you've told me about your current financial situation if something happens to you and you're not insured your family would have to sell the family home to pay off the $400,000 mortgage.

Before we get into the answer to this, I want you to note that in both situations the insurance payout is $400,000. In both situations, the premium that would have to be paid is $76 per month. So, those two things are the same.

Let's consider what's different.

Benefits vs. Problems – The first difference is the way the outcome of an insurance event is framed. In Statement A the outcome is framed as a benefit. The benefit of the insurance is the payment of $400,000 to the family of the insured. In Statement B, the outcome is framed as a problem that would be experienced. The problem being the need to sell the family home to pay out a mortgage of $400,000.

Future Situation/Insured vs. Current Situation/Uninsured – In Statement A, what is said focuses the customer's mind on what their family would experience in the future if the insurance was in place. In Statement B, the statement focuses the customer's mind on their current situation (a $400,000 mortgage on the family home) and what the family would experience if the insurance was not in place.

Gains vs. Losses – A final difference is that in Statement A the benefit is framed as something the family would gain following an insurance event. In statement B the problem is framed as something the family would lose following an insurance event.

WHAT DOES THE RESEARCH TELL US?

I'm going to keep this as light as possible, but as an insurance professional you need to understand how people make decisions. This will ensure the way you sell insurance is consistent with people making choices to take the right amount of cover.

The framing effect tells us that the way we present the value of taking insurance cover is likely to impact the choices made by the person we are speaking to. This effect has consistently been proven to be one of the strongest biases in decision making.[1]

In one study[2], two sets of PhD students were asked to register early for their courses. A saving (benefit) was framed as a discount for early registration to the first group. For the second group, the same amount of saving was framed as avoiding a penalty (problem) for late registration. In both scenarios, the financial benefit was the same, but the problem-focused group had almost a 40% higher rate of early registration.

In another study funded by the Pacific Energy Group, two sales teams selling insulation were given two different strategies. The team provided with a problem-focused set of sales strategies were taught how to focus the customer on problems rather than benefits, experienced sales results almost double that of the team using benefit-focused strategies.[3]

Kahnemann and Tversky's study on loss aversion[4] tells us people are more likely to be motivated to avoid a $400,000 loss than they are to chase a $400,000 gain. Some studies have suggested that framing around loss can have twice the psychological impact on decision making compared to framing the same outcome around benefit or gain.[5]

If we compare Statement A to Statement B, it would be fair to suggest that Statement B would be significantly more likely to cause a person to decide on taking cover because:

- It frames the cover of $400,000 as a strategy for avoiding loss (selling the family home) rather than a strategy for gaining a payment (a $400,000 payout).

- It frames the cover of $400,000 as a strategy for solving a problem (the risk the family would have to sell the house).

- It frames the risk around something personal (the family home and the family's living situation).

- It relates the risk to something current and tangible (the $400,000 mortgage).

Put simply, we are significantly more motivated to avoid a loss than we are to gain a benefit. This means that we will be significantly more successful if the way that we engage people in the insurance conversation focuses them on the problems they need to solve rather than the benefits of your insurance products.

HOW DO YOU EXPLAIN THE PROBLEMS LIFE INSURANCE CAN SOLVE?

Before you read on, take a little time out to think this through at a deep level. When someone asks you

"Why would I need life insurance?"

how effectively are you responding? Whether you have accreditation to provide specific advice or not, your ability to explain this is at the core of your ability to protect and provide for those you engage in the insurance conversation.

We know that people are more likely to emotionally respond to (and act on) solving a problem than they are to take advantage of a benefit. So consider the following response, which is unfortunately all too common.

"Well, if you die your family or loved ones get paid out a sum of money that you've insured yourself for."

I'm hoping after reading the last few pages you can figure out the problem with this sort of statement, but let me spell it out anyway. The problems with this statement include:

- It mentions "death", which to most humans is an abstract concept they find easy to discount, deny or just plain ignore.

- It mentions money, which once again for most people is an abstract concept. What I mean by that is when most people think of money, they don't have an emotional reaction until they connect it to doing something with the money.

The point here is that this type of response is highly unlikely to put a person in a state of mind that makes them more likely to seriously consider either purchasing insurance or re-evaluating whether they have enough insurance. We can do better. Let me explain how I suggest you do that.

THREE CORE PROBLEMS LIFE INSURANCE SOLVES

There are three core problems life insurance can help a person solve, and the more you understand and empathise with these problems, the more effective you'll be in the insurance conversation.

1. **Avoiding Burdening Loved Ones** – The first problem life insurance solves is making sure that if a person dies, they don't leave behind or create debts that burden their loved ones. If

a policy has TPD, a payout on disability or terminal diagnosis, this ensures they don't burden their loved ones with the costs associated with caring for them.

2. **Avoiding Diminished Lifestyle for Loved Ones** – Following the death of a partner many families are left in a situation where the income coming into the household is significantly diminished. There's often also significant extra costs involved in caring for children due to the surviving partner having to work and care for children as a single parent.

3. **Lack of Funds to Leave a Legacy** – Most people with families and loved ones would like to leave behind funds that enable things like payment for a deposit on a home, payment of school or university fees or just some extra money to make life easier. While most would like to do this, few have sufficient wealth to ensure it will happen if they die.

HOW YOU SHOULD EXPLAIN THE VALUE OF LIFE INSURANCE

The next time someone asks you why they might need life insurance, this is my suggested response.

"People buy life insurance for different reasons, but there tend to be three common reasons. The first is to make sure they don't leave behind any debts that would burden their family or loved ones. A common debt people want to get rid of is a mortgage on the family home.

The second reason is making sure their family's lifestyle isn't harmed by their death. When most people add up the cost of paying all their bills, they realise their family would have to downsize their lifestyle if their income was no longer being paid.

And the third reason isn't as common as the first two, but some people just want to leave money behind for people they love. Sometimes that's for things like paying a deposit on a home or covering university and school fees.

So – if something did happen to you, which of those three would be most important?"

Why is this better?

- It focuses people on tangible aspects of their current life like debts, the family home, the mortgage on the family home, their current income, paying bills, helping their children and ensuring their children aren't left in debt because of studying.

- It gives them options and enables them to make a choice.

- It asks them to consider which aspect is most important to them and associates having life insurance with avoiding painful consequences of death.

ENGAGING CUSTOMERS AROUND PROBLEMS AT A DEEPER LEVEL

One of the biggest challenges most insurance salespeople have is that they've never experienced the dramatic impact of under-insurance when a loved one dies. I can appreciate it's a dark concept, but the more you understand all the potential consequences in detail, the more motivated you will be to protect and provide for all those you engage in insurance conversations. This understanding will often make those discussions richer and more meaningful for the other person and help them truly understand the consequences of failing to have adequate cover in place.

So, before we move forward, I want to take a little time out to make sure we all understand what those consequences are or could be. I want to acknowledge that this list obviously ignores the mental cost and consequences of losing a loved one and these are often more challenging than the financial costs and consequences. Having said that, lumping financial burden and distress on top of those often makes it harder for loved ones and families to effectively move through the grieving process.

So the dollar costs and consequences are important.

I also need to acknowledge that through some smart structuring, the insured's assets can be protected from some of the consequences I'll outline below. But in general, this sort of legal structuring is only affordable and relevant for those that don't have a high need for insurance. For most of you selling insurance, we can and should assume that all the consequences I outline below are relevant and should be brought to the attention of the person we're speaking to.

This is not meant to be a complete list, but it will give you a firm grounding in exactly what you're protecting loved ones from and how the insurance you sell today can and will provide for the loved ones of the insured.

BURDENING
LOVED ONES WITH DEBT
LEFT BEHIND

- **Mortgages** – Few families have the luxury of complete home ownership, and most homeowners in need of insurance will leave behind a mortgage on the family home. In most cases, the loss of the insured's income will mean the mortgage payments are extremely difficult to pay or outside the budget of loved ones left behind. This means that on top of losing a father, mother or partner the family will need to sell the family home and downsize. This is something I went through and while I'm incredibly proud of my mother for putting a great roof over my head, it was a challenge to move out of a lovely family home into an apartment.

- **Funeral Costs** – If you don't know how much funerals cost, I'm confident you'll be surprised to know that even a relatively basic burial is going to cost a family $6,000–8,000 and more likely close to $12,000. There are a lot of people that simply don't have that much cash available on short notice and the guilt associated with not being able to host the funeral you want for the departed is often significant. None of us would want to leave that sort of stress behind but so many do because they just didn't think about it.

- **Car Finance** – Other than the family home, a car is the largest purchase most households will make and that generally means financing the majority or all the cost of the car. As we all know, when you drive a car off the lot it significantly diminishes in value. So, if that car needs to be sold, there's often a gap between the sales price and the amount of money that needs to be paid to the finance company from the insured's estate. When my father was murdered, his car was also stolen. Unfortunately, the insurance on the car had recently expired, and finance on a car that couldn't be found or sold was another debt my mother had to deal with out of the estate.

- **Other Finance** – We live in an age where people can and do finance almost everything. Something that's common is "no interest loans" and while these can be very effective strategies for buying things like furniture and household goods there's one risk that becomes highly relevant when a partner in a marriage dies. If a payment is missed on many of these loans penalty interest at an incredibly high rate is applied to the loan. Guess what often happens when families are both grieving the death of a loved one and facing financial challenges? You guessed it – payments get missed.

- **Credit Cards** – Interest on the 16 million credit cards Australians hold was over $30 billion in 2016! In the USA, average credit card debt per household is just over $16,000.[6] With over 70% of Australians[7] holding a credit card there is a very high probability debt on a credit card will be left behind and need to be paid out of the insured's estate. These cards are often jointly held, and if there's no money in the estate, the partner is left behind with the debt.

And if that's not paid off quickly, the interest on that debt is extremely high.

DEATH RESULTING IN DRAMATIC LIFESTYLE CHANGES

Some people will not have any debt, but that doesn't mean insurance isn't an important and necessary tool they need to use to genuinely protect and provide for those they love.

- **Family Home Expense** – If you don't have a mortgage because you rent the family home, your family is still going to need to live somewhere after you die. And that means they must pay rent, utilities and all the other expenses, associated with putting a roof over their heads. If the insured's income was a major contributor to family expenses, this would mean they're going to have to downsize where the family lives and possibly move away from family and friends.

- **Burdening the Extended Family** – Some will assume that their loved ones could live with parents or other members of the extended family. There are three big problems with this assumption. First, if that assumption is wrong, they have nowhere to live. Second, if your loved ones really wanted to live with their or the insured's extended family, they would probably be doing it now. And third, even if the extended family is willing to accommodate the loved ones left behind, they probably didn't plan on being part of the insurance policy and are likely to face financial pressures for their generosity.

- **Living Expenses** – When a parent dies, living expenses like food, travel and entertainment generally don't drop by very much. The problem with this is that when you ask most people how much disposable income they have left each month after expenses, there's very little saving going on. What does drop dramatically in many situations is the amount of income coming into the household to pay those expenses. If this is the case, the insured's family is likely to go from "what's on at the movies this weekend" to "what haven't we watched on Netflix". This might sound like a First World problem, but once again these sorts of changes make the grieving process for those left behind even more challenging.

- **School Expenses** – A significant number of children go to private schools that cost a lot of money. The loss of the insured's income is often the difference between being able to pay school fees and sending the children to a local school. I went to one of those local schools, but the last thing I would have wanted to do after my father passed away was leave a school full of the amazing friends that provided such incredible support to me following the death of my father.

- **Surviving Parent Needing to Work** – For families the death of a partner involves personal grieving, supporting others through their grieving and a significant administrative hassle of finalising the insured's estate. In all the examples above I've assumed the surviving partner had a job, but in many situations, they don't and find themselves needing to get a job to generate income. This is not something they want to do urgently. Unfortunately it's often something they must do urgently, because of financial stress. It is also often the case in this situation that they're unable to earn the same income as the insured and that makes it even more emotionally challenging.

LACK OF
A LEGACY

- This might seem like a First World problem, but the death of a parent will often result in those dreams of paying the children's university fees or helping them into their first home disappear rapidly. This is something the surviving parent must live with, and their children's debts are often a reminder of the loved one they lost. Not ideal. Interestingly, I recently read research suggesting this is the second most common reason for purchasing insurance, ahead of reasons like replacing lost income and paying off the mortgage!

Forget about yourself for a moment. Most of us just can't effectively conceptualise our parents' dying and the impact that would have on the family if that were to occur.

Instead, I want you to choose a close friend or family member that has a young family. Imagine all the above happening to them because of the loss of their partner. Take some time out to read through each of the problems I've outlined and really spend some time thinking about how you would feel if a close friend or sibling lost their partner and they were underinsured. Take some time out to think through how much financial capacity you and your family have to make all those problems go away.

This is a reality for many families that lose someone uninsured or underinsured. This is why protecting and providing through the sale of insurance is a truly heroic act. This is what you need to remind yourself of every day as you're walking to work.

WHY DON'T PEOPLE BUY ENOUGH COVER?

Before we move on to the skills you need to make sure none of this happens to people you have the insurance conversation with, let's take a quick moment out to consider why people don't buy or fail to buy enough insurance.

If you've really read what I've shared above and really thought about, it makes absolutely no sense for most people to be roaming around the world in an uninsured or underinsured state. The more you understand the reasons people are not buying more cover, the better you get at helping them understand why this is not an acceptable situation. This understanding will also help you understand why it's so important to be ethically persuasive and deliberate as you help a person through their insurance purchasing journey and present the case for acting to purchase the right amount of cover.

This is not a complete list of all the reasons people fail to put adequate cover in place, but it will give you the understanding you need for the purposes of this book.

- **Assumptions on existing amount of cover through Superannuation or Group Cover** – People generally underestimate how much cover they need and overestimate how much cover is contained in their superannuation or group cover policy. This is an extremely common objection, but it is very rare for a person using this objection to be able to specifically tell you how much cover they have under those policies.

- **Ignorance of their loved ones' financial exposure** – An extremely common question asked by prospective customer is,

"How much cover do I need?"

When an effective and compliant strategy that helps a potential purchaser quantify their needs is used, most people are surprised at just how much cover is required to meet all their wishes upon an insurance event occurring.

- **Lack of trust in the ability to claim** – Let's not beat around the bush, the insurance industry does not have a great brand in most countries. Whether this is justified or not is irrelevant. The statistics tell us that a major reason for not buying more cover is a lack of trust that it will be paid to loved ones upon an insurance event.

- **The perception that it's too expensive** – In several studies the research suggests that many people estimate the cost of insurance at more than double the actual cost. People don't bother engaging because they incorrectly believe the amount they need and want is not within their budget.

- **Overconfidence in the ability to self-insure** – In Western culture we're generally not great at taking financial care of our extended families. We're so stretched with consumerism and keeping up with the Joneses that even if we wanted to, we can't afford to. People think that having $500,000 equity in their home means their family will be fine, but they forget that after they're gone, their family will need somewhere to live!

- **Bad experience with an insurance salesperson** – In general, the way insurance is sold does not represent the industry you work in as a true profession. I can appreciate you may be offended by that comment, but to the public the research shows too many people have been SOLD insurance rather than being helped through their purchasing journey.

Other reasons include the fact that there's no legal requirement to insure yourself, lack of understanding in the value of insurance, fear and discomfort with death, discomfort with the underwriting process, the perception that they're not eligible, delusions of immortality and being too busy to get around to it. In some cultures, it's even considered bad luck to buy insurance!

As I mentioned before, this means you need to be confident in leveraging ethical influence strategies and education to move people past these excuses. That takes us to the next chapter and the PAVE Principle.

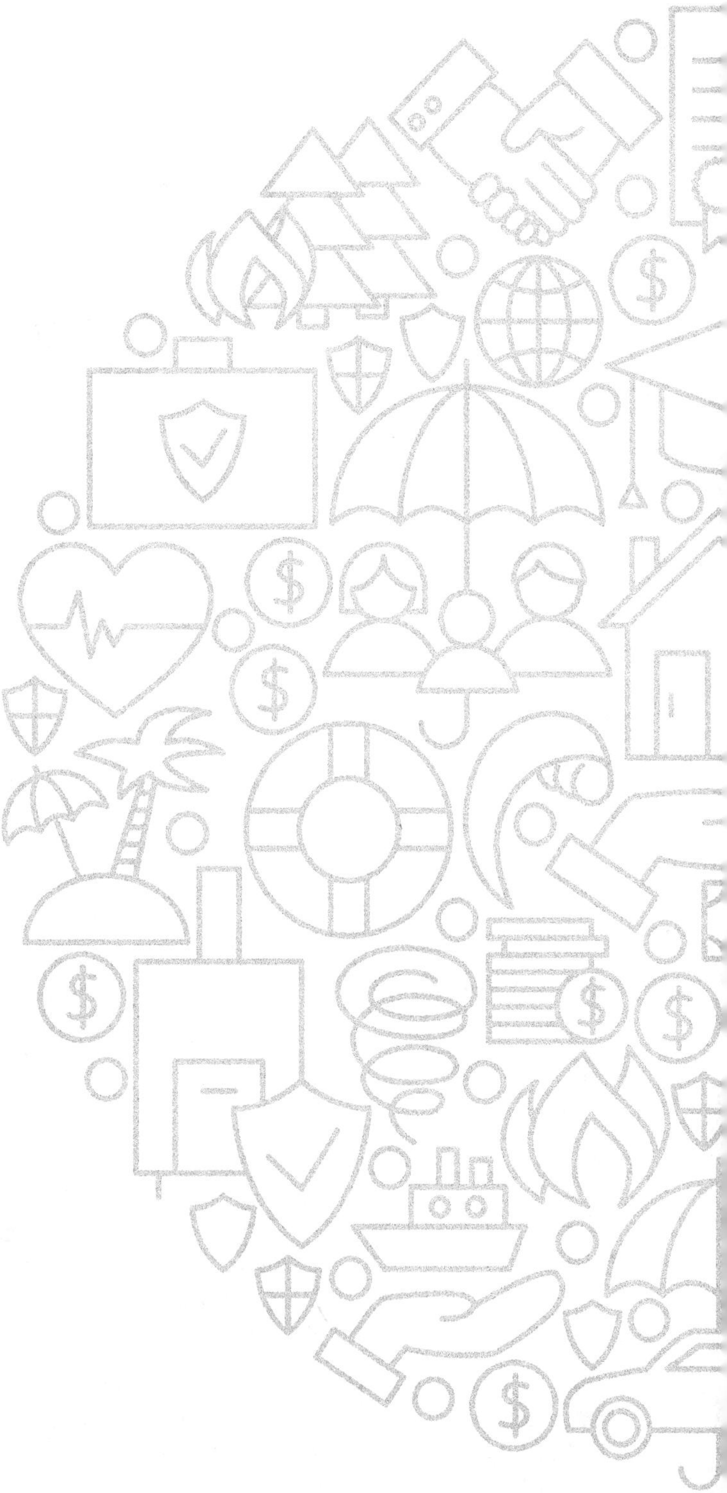

CHAPTER THREE

THE PAVE PRINCIPLE

The PAVE Principle tells us that two things will drive the likelihood a person will or won't insure the risk in their life. Those two drivers are the person's acknowledgement of the problems (risk and pain) they face if an insurance event occurs and the value (benefits) they expect to achieve, if they purchase insurance cover. It can best be explained by considering the following diagram.

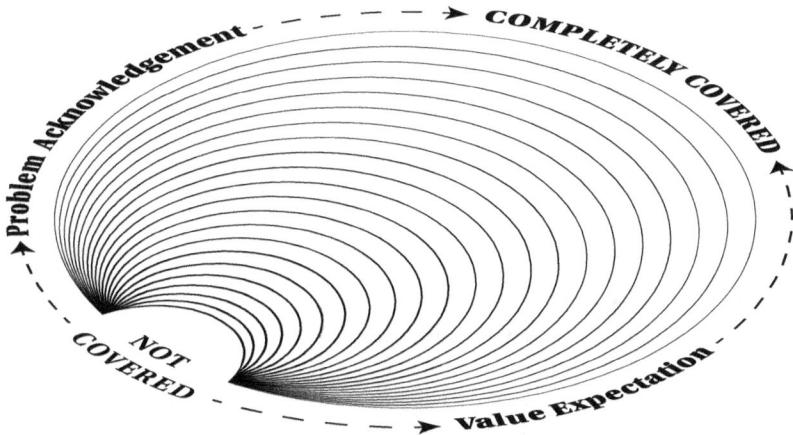

In an ideal world, every customer would be completely aware of all the problems associated with being underinsured. Not only would they be aware, but they would also acknowledge that those were problems for them personally. The higher this awareness and acknowledgement, the more likely it is that a person will be motivated to seek the right amount of cover.

But awareness and even acknowledgement on their own, are not enough. I have no doubt that all of you have experienced people that know they need insurance and acknowledge their risk exposure but just can't seem to justify the expense of premiums.

The challenge here is that their expectation of value is low. That dramatically reduces their motivation to pay for cover. One of the most challenging things about selling insurance compared to other products, is the lack of an immediate benefit or value. For a person to receive the full possible value a policy could provide, they would have to make a claim, and that's something we (and they) don't want to happen!

Having said that, the more value a person experiences in their insurance purchasing journey and the more value they expect in the event they do purchase the right cover, the more motivated they'll be to buy the right cover.

We can frame this up as a mathematical equation:

$$\textbf{PA} \times \textbf{VE} = \textbf{MC}$$

Problem Acknowledgement	Value Expectation	Motivation to Cover

The reason there is a multiplication symbol in the equation, is to remind you that both PA and VE need to be high, if you expect customers to be motivated to cover the risk in their lives.

To truly be a customer-centric expert in insurance sales, you need to have a highly developed understanding of the problems solved by the insurance you sell, an ability to help people acknowledge they (and their families) face those problems and an ability to help people understand and experience the value of covering their risk to solve those problems. The higher the level of Problem Acknowledgement and Value Expectation the more likely it is that Motivation to Cover will be high.

Let's consider what drives higher levels of Problem Acknowledgement and Value Expectation.

PROBLEM ACKNOWLEDGEMENT

People don't buy insurance policies. They buy a solution to the problems they and their loved ones will experience when they die or if they become totally and permanently disabled.

Until a person acknowledges these problems, they won't perceive there's a need for the insurance you sell. So, to be an expert in your product you need to have an expert knowledge of all the problems your customers face if they fail to provide adequate cover for themselves and those they love. And once you understand what those problems are, you need to develop the skills required to the help customers become aware of, understand and acknowledge these problems.

At a base level, the reason we need to leverage Problem Acknowledgement strategies is to make it clear that a failure to act will result in significant problems if an insurance event occurs. If we do this ethically and with empathy, the person we're speaking to will be thinking and feeling that there will be a significant problem if something happens and they're uninsured or underinsured.

When selling insurance, there are 10 strategies we can use to heighten a customer's awareness, acceptance, understanding and commitment to resolving problems rather than resolving an issue. The more effectively and ethically we execute these strategies, the more likely it becomes the customer will act to ensure they have adequate cover in place for their circumstances.

1. Increasing a person's awareness of the problems associated with no insurance/underinsurance

2. Helping a person consider the relevance of those problems to their personal circumstances

3. Promoting acknowledgement that current insurance cover or no insurance is a real and current problem

4. Helping a customer consider the financial cost for loved ones if they fail to insure and an insurance event occurs

5. Helping a customer consider the consequences that would flow from financial problems associated with failure to insure if an insurance event occurs

6. Including engagement of other family members in the insurance conversation

7. Helping a customer quantify the costs/consequences of the problem(s) they have accepted and considered

8. Gaining voluntary and specific commitments consistent with the need for adequate cover

9. Gaining a commitment to solve those problems shared with loved ones

10. Encouragement to make a covered/uncovered or underinsured decision

VALUE
EXPECTATION

People don't object to the price of your insurance. They object because they don't perceive the value that adequate cover will provide is greater than the price they must pay.

Life insurance offers no immediate value, and that means you need to deliberately assist customers to understand and experience value throughout their insurance purchasing journey. The more value a customer experiences throughout their purchasing journey, the more likely it becomes that they'll be motivated to purchase adequate cover.

At a base level, the reason we need to leverage Value Expectation strategies is to help the person understand that purchasing the right amount of cover will result in significant benefits and value. If we do this ethically and with confidence, the person we're speaking to will be thinking and feeling that the price they must pay for insurance is significantly less than the price their loved ones will pay if something happens and they're uninsured or underinsured.

Value is a perception, and that means it's more about the thoughts and emotions the customer experiences than the price that's on your quote. When selling insurance, there are 10 strategies we can use to increase a person's perception of the value they will receive by purchasing insurance from us.

When you do this effectively throughout the customer's insurance purchasing journey, you'll increase the probability that their price sensitivity is diminished and their perception of value is heightened.

1. Building top-of-mind awareness of the availability of cover
2. Building confidence that insurance paid for will deliver the cover required should an insurance event occur
3. Doing the hard work (underwriting) with the customer to confirm their eligibility for cover and the level of cover they're able to access
4. Gaining confirmation that the cost of premiums can be paid from the customer's current budget

5. Building a sense of reciprocity for educating, assisting and delivering great service throughout the insurance purchasing journey

6. Gaining a voluntary and specific commitment that confirms the purchase of insurance is consistent with the person's goals/values/other purchases/actions

7. Helping the customer make a favourable comparison with alternative options/other purchases and expenses

8. Developing a personal commitment from the customer to the value of their relationship with the salesperson

9. Gaining a voluntary commitment that the cost of premiums is outweighed by the value of being fully covered

10. Guiding the customer to mentally and emotionally experiencing the peace of mind that having their insurance affairs in order will deliver

BUYING VS. BEING SOLD

In the following two chapters I'll explain each of these in more detail and give you an example of how you can achieve each one in your sales process. The big point I want to make here is that if you can achieve each of these in your sales process, people won't feel like they've been sold insurance. Instead, they'll feel like they've bought insurance and your role was guiding them rather than selling them.

Using the PAVE Principle within your sales process will also dramatically improve customer understanding of the need for insurance without the need for making statements or providing advice. And that is going to both help the customers you sell to and ethically improve your conversion.

CHAPTER FOUR

PROBLEM ACKNOWLEDGEMENT – HOW TO TRIGGER CONCERN

At the core of Problem Acknowledgement is the need to ethically create a level of concern that makes failure to act uncomfortable. We need people to be more concerned about not buying insurance than they are about the effort they'll need to put into the insurance purchasing journey and the expense of ongoing premiums. I'll come back to these strategies as we move through how to ethically apply the ROI Sales Methodology in following chapters.

In some of the examples I provide, the imaginary person we're selling to is Bill. In the examples, he's the primary income earner. I want to acknowledge here that in many families the female partner is the primary income earner. I also want to remind all of you to never assume it's the male. While I'm reminding you not to make assumptions, another one to avoid is assuming a person's partner is the opposite sex.

In this chapter and the next, I'll give you a deeper explanation and example of each of them before we move on to the ROI Sales Methodology.

STRATEGY #1

INCREASING A PERSON'S AWARENESS OF THE PROBLEMS ASSOCIATED WITH NO INSURANCE/UNDERINSURANCE

People are very good at mentally deleting anything that makes them uncomfortable and that includes their death.

If you don't like your weight, you stay off the scales and avoid that pair of jeans that just don't fit anymore. If you're a smoker, I can bet that you can't tell me what the health warning is on your packet of cigarettes. Those of us who enjoy a drink a little too much generally underestimate how many drinks we had the night before. And I could go on, but the point I want to make is that we're very good at deleting and even denying any information that might make us feel uncomfortable.

So, just the act of including and highlighting potential problems into your insurance conversations will increase the probability of action.

A good example of this is using the strategy I shared on how to explain why people buy insurance. I'll shorten this to provide you with an example of increasing awareness of the problems.

"Bill, there are three major reasons people generally purchase insurance. One of the big ones is making

sure that the loss of their income doesn't mean the family has to dramatically downsize their lifestyle..."

As you can see from this example, I've raised Bill's awareness of a problem he should be considering – whether his family's lifestyle would suffer if his income was no longer available due to an insurance event.

STRATEGY #2

HELPING A PERSON CONSIDER THE RELEVANCE OF THOSE PROBLEMS TO THEIR PERSONAL CIRCUMSTANCES

As I've noted earlier, many people are simply ignorant of all the problems that would flow from an insurance event.

But even people who do understand the three major reasons for needing insurance often discount them as not being relevant to their personal circumstances. If you can't provide advice, you're not able to tell them these problems are relevant to their circumstances. But you can guide them to that realisation by asking great questions.

If we go back to our lifestyle problem, an example of this would be a question like the following.

"What would your family have to stop spending on, if your income wasn't available?"

Another version of this would be,

"How long do you think your family could maintain the current spending and lifestyle if your income wasn't coming into the household?"

And one final example might be,

"Bill, I read an interesting statistic suggesting one in three households would have immediate problems paying household expenses if the primary income was no longer coming into the household. How long do you think your family could continue to spend at the current rate?"

The point here is that we're taking the problem from a concept, to a relevant concern, by asking the prospective customer to consider how the problem relates to their personal circumstances.

STRATEGY #3

PROMOTING ACKNOWLEDGEMENT THAT CURRENT INSURANCE COVER OR NO INSURANCE IS A REAL AND CURRENT PROBLEM

Until the person you're selling to acknowledges that there's a problem, what you're selling is not a solution.

Even where people understand the personal relevance, they're often in denial that the problem is a real one or that it deserves immediate attention. Our goal is to create as high a level of problem acknowledgement as possible.

The next level of Problem Acknowledgment is achieved by asking the prospective customer to confirm this is a problem.

Once again, we do this with questions rather than statements, and an example would be a question like this.

"And Bill, I can appreciate it's not the most comfortable thing to think about. But would you want them to have to downsize their lifestyle if

something did happen to you or your ability to earn income?"

What we're doing here is ethically compelling the person we're engaging to seriously consider whether there's a problem they need to seriously consider. This is an incredibly important part of a person's insurance purchasing journey. The more we can help people accept there's a problem to fix the more engaged they'll be in exploring insurance solutions with us.

STRATEGY #4

HELPING A CUSTOMER CONSIDER THE FINANCIAL COST FOR LOVED ONES IF THEY FAIL TO INSURE AND AN INSURANCE EVENT OCCURS

The line between costs and consequences (Strategy #5) is a blurred one, so don't get too hung up on whether something is a cost or a consequence. In general, a cost will be able to be quantified in dollar terms. A consequence will generally be an indirect problem that flows from a cost. As an example, mortgage payments are a cost that will need to be borne by the surviving partner. If they can't make those payments, a consequence will be the need to sell the family home.

The clearer the costs are in the mind of the purchaser, the more real the problem becomes and the more compelled they feel to do something about it. An example of how we move into this part of the insurance conversation would be a question like this.

"Have you considered how much it costs to run your household each year?"

STRATEGY #5

HELPING A CUSTOMER CONSIDER THE CONSEQUENCES THAT WOULD FLOW FROM FINANCIAL PROBLEMS ASSOCIATED WITH FAILURE TO INSURE IF AN INSURANCE EVENT OCCURS

As I said before, people are good at mentally deleting the problems that make them feel uncomfortable. Research tells us they're even better at completely ignoring the consequences that may flow from those problems. In Charles Dickens' book *A Christmas Carol*, the main character, Ebenezer Scrooge is forced to confront what his life will look like in the future if he fails to change his behaviour.

The more we help a person experience the dire consequences of failing to protect and provide for their family, the more likely it is that we will transform them into someone that cares about insurance enough to act today.

If we go back to our example, the following question will cause Bill to consider the consequences of inadequate cover.

"Bill, if your income wasn't available to Mary and the kids, where do you think they could cut down expenditure to make ends meet?"

Neuroscience is telling us that when people visualise emotional experiences in graphic detail, there is little difference between the visualisation and experiencing the real event. The more you can ethically and empathetically take a person on a journey into the future without insurance, the more emotionally committed they'll be to accepting and doing something about the consequences of inadequate cover for those they love.

STRATEGY #6

INCLUDING ENGAGEMENT OF OTHER FAMILY MEMBERS IN THE INSURANCE CONVERSATION

The problems associated with inadequate cover become significantly more real when they're discussed with a partner or dependent child.

Saying out loud,

"There's a problem that needs to be fixed."

is the first level of Problem Acknowledgement. Saying to a partner,

"There's a problem we need to fix."

takes it to another level.

I'm not promoting the use of this strategy, but let me share an example of a strategy that was commonly used in the industry in years gone by, when the husband was almost always the primary income earner.

The unsuspecting couple would agree, and the conversation would start with the advisor saying something like:

"Mary. Bill has just died. Do you have enough cash in the bank to pay for the funeral?"

In most cases, Bill would try to answer the question, but before he could, the advisor would say:

"Please stop answering the question Bill. You're dead."

The advisor would then turn to Mary and ask the question again. This would go on for three to four uncomfortable questions at which point a few things had happened.

It was very clear to Bill that Mary and the family would suffer if something happened to him. And it was also very clear that Mary was not happy about the situation.

Once again, I do *not* endorse this strategy. What I do endorse is asking people to speak to their partners about the problems that are identified through the initial discussion.

Where you're only speaking to one of the partners, asking to engage the other partner may seem like it will slow down the sale. As a customer-centric salesperson, that shouldn't concern you. In my experience it is more likely to speed up decision making and make a cancellation significantly less likely. It's also the protect and provide way.

You should want couples to be clear about the problems and risks they face if an event happens to either of them. You should be passionate about making sure both partners are educated to support each other in making smarter choices today, to protect each other's future. Just the act of letting a partner know you're considering insurance, increases the level of Problem Acknowledgement.

STRATEGY #7

HELPING A CUSTOMER QUANTIFY THE COSTS/CONSEQUENCES OF THE PROBLEM(S) THEY HAVE ACCEPTED AND CONSIDERED

Another by-product of getting a couple together to discuss their insurance needs is that it often results in the quantification of emotional concerns that haven't been discussed. Many couples avoid a discussion about insurance and the reasons for that are numerous. But when the conversation does happen, at least one of the partners is generally surprised by the level of concern the other partner has around being inadequately covered. Helping couples bring this to the surface enables them to jointly quantify just how much concern there is, and that increases the probability of action.

Some of the research I've seen at conferences suggests that while funding retirement is people's number one financial concern, very few have ever completed a detailed quantification of how much money they'll need to fund their retirement. This avoidance relates to the fact that as we quantify a problem, it becomes much more real and much more uncomfortable to ignore.

So, the more we can help a person quantify their exact need, the more real the problem becomes and the more they acknowledge the problem. As an example, let me share a string of questions and answers that would enable Bill and Mary to more effectively quantify their problems and by doing so, educate them on how much insurance they need without offering any advice.

SALESPERSON *"Bill is it OK to ask you a few questions that might help you understand how much insurance you would need to make sure Mary and the kids didn't have to downsize their lifestyle?"*

BILL "Sure."

SALESPERSON *"Do you think Mary would be able to earn a higher income if she changed roles or worked an extra job?"*

BILL "I wouldn't want her to have to work an extra job. She might be able to earn a bit more, but not much."

SALESPERSON *"OK. So, for the purposes of this conversation, we'll assume her income remains the same. Would you want her to be able to take some time out from work if something did happen to you?"*

BILL "I guess so."

SALESPERSON *"Is there a particular amount of time you would want her to be able to take off having to work?"*

BILL "I think about six months."

SALESPERSON *"OK. So, her income wouldn't be available for six months assuming she could get that much time off. How much would six months of her income be?"*

BILL "About $25,000."

SALESPERSON *"OK. So, I can't advise you on the amount of cover you need but would you want to cover that $25,000?"*

BILL "Yes."

SALESPERSON *"What about your income. There are two things to consider here. How much do you earn and how much is left over at the end of each month after the household expenses are paid?"*

BILL "I earn $85,000 a year after tax, and we save about $5,000 a year."

SALESPERSON *"OK, that's great. So, if we just focus on the income you bring into the household, there is about $80,000 of expenses that would need to be covered per year?"*

BILL "Sounds about right."

SALESPERSON *"Have you thought about how many years Mary would need that sort of money? Something a lot of people use when they consider this, is how long it will be before the kids are out of school. But that's just one consideration, and it's up to you. How many years would you want to allow for?"*

BILL "I think about three years would be fine."

SALESPERSON *"Great. So, if we take three years at $80,000, that's $240,000. If we add the $25,000 for Mary not earning an income for 6 months that's a total of $265,000 that's required to maintain the current lifestyle for three years. Does that sound about right to you?"*

I suggest an important point here is that if you asked Bill how much Mary will need to run the house, he would be very likely to come up with a much smaller amount. Please take note, I'm not trying to increase the amount of insurance Bill buys. I'm trying to make sure the process he uses to assess how much is needed is based on the facts of his life. I'm also making sure that his problem acknowledgement is heightened by turning the concept of ongoing lifestyle into a quantified number of dollars.

Remember that I also want to help him quantify the consequences. The type of question I might ask following quantifying the cost of underinsurance is something like,

"If Mary didn't have access to extra money to cover household expenses what would she have to sacrifice to make ends meet?"

If this sounds a little cruel, I'm not going to apologise. What's truly cruel is when an insurance event occurs, and these costs and consequences become a reality because there's inadequate insurance in place.

STRATEGY #8

GAINING VOLUNTARY AND SPECIFIC COMMITMENTS CONSISTENT WITH THE NEED FOR ADEQUATE COVER

When we make a commitment, we experience a subconscious compulsion to act in a manner consistent with that commitment.

Before I share examples of how this can and should be used in the insurance conversation, let me share a few details of an experiment that will help you understand this concept more easily.

Getting someone to buy adequate cover can be challenging. But I suggest getting someone to risk personal harm to protect your possessions is an even more difficult sell.

But this is exactly what psychologist Thomas Moriarty achieved in what's known as the "beach blanket" experiment.

The researchers had a researcher place their beach towel approximately 5 feet from another person (the bystander), place a radio on the towel and then go for a swim. Another researcher would then walk over to the towel and steal the radio. Under these circumstances, only four out of 20 bystanders said or did anything.

Then they changed one thing and one thing only. Before going for a swim, the first researcher would ask the bystander to mind their valuables while they went for a swim. Under these circumstances, 19 out of 20 bystanders said and did something to protect the first researcher's (a stranger) radio.

What the research showed was that when someone made a commitment to protect the radio, they felt significantly more compelled to act in a manner consistent with that commitment and protect the radio from theft.

Other research has shown that the more voluntary or specific the commitment, the more likely it is that people will feel compelled to behave in a consistent manner. So, the more effective we are in gaining voluntary and specific commitments that protecting and providing for loved ones is important to the person we're speaking to, the more subconsciously they will feel compelled to purchase adequate cover. This dynamic also means they will feel uncomfortable with doing things that are inconsistent with this commitment, like purchasing inadequate cover or remaining uncovered.

If we go back to our example, a question that may gain the sort of commitment we're looking for would be as follows:

"Bill, you mentioned the family home before. How important is it that your family can stay in the home if something happens to your income?"

Or another following the,

"What would the family have to sacrifice?"

part of the conversation might be,

"What's non-negotiable for you Bill? What would you want them not to have to sacrifice?"

Once again, we're using questions and not statements. This is particularly important in relation to this strategy. Making a statement like,

"Keeping a roof over the family's head is obviously important."

is very different to the person you're speaking with telling you that it is important to them (a voluntary commitment).

Making a statement like,

"And Mary could use the insurance to pay household expenses."

is very different to Bill telling you, "The household costs about $80,000 a year to run (a specific commitment) and I wouldn't want anything to change (a voluntary commitment)."

STRATEGY #9

GAINING A COMMITMENT TO SOLVE THOSE PROBLEMS SHARED WITH LOVED ONES

As you can see from the beach blanket experiment, a commitment can have a dramatic impact on a person's compulsion for consistent behaviour. One other aspect of commitment is whether the commitment is a public and shared commitment or whether it is a commitment that is only internalised by the person.

Our desire to be seen as a person that keeps their word to those we love is very strong. Another way of saying this is that when you make a commitment to someone you love you're significantly more likely to follow through on it. This is another reason I promote doing whatever it takes to engage a person's partner in the insurance conversation.

STRATEGY #10

ENCOURAGEMENT TO MAKE A COVERED/UNCOVERED OR UNDERCOVERED DECISION

There is only one thing worse than an underinsured person, ignorant about the risk their loved ones face each day. That's an underinsured person that has been educated about their insurance needs and has procrastinated on deciding whether to cover that risk or not.

One of the reasons that people procrastinate is because insurance salespeople fail to create a dynamic that compels them to decide either way. If you make achieving a decision, either way, more important than making a sale, you'll sleep better at night, and you'll help more people make the decisions they need to make. If you're happy to take an "I'll think about it", then there is absolutely no problem for the person you're speaking to if they fail to decide. This enables them to head back out into the world, exposed to all the risks that could cause an insurance event, without deciding. Procrastinating on an insurance decision does not magically ward off car crashes, cancer, heart attacks and other things that are going to be life changing for the person you're speaking to and their loved ones.

An example of a strategy that you might use to promote a decision either way is as follows.

> **BILL** "Thanks for all your time. I want to take all that away and think about it."

> **SALESPERSON** *"I understand the premiums are higher than you expected Bill but that relates to the risks you've identified through our conversation. And those risks aren't going to go away. My preference is to put the cover in place for you from today and then allow you to cancel or change the policy next week when you've thought about it some more. Can we get that cover in place for you before you leave the office Bill?"*

> **BILL** "I hear what you're saying, but I just need time to think."

> **SALESPERSON** *"My job isn't to force you to take out insurance Bill. It's to educate you on the risks and to give you information to help you make better decisions. Can we lock in a specific time next week for me to call you? I promise I won't do a hard sell. All I want to know is whether your choice is to cover the risk we've discussed or not. The last thing I want is your wife calling me to find out why you're not insured and having to tell her we were in the "think about it" phase of the conversation. What time Monday will work for you, Bill?"*

I have no doubt some genius from your sales enablement team is saying,

"Don't do it that way. Handle the objection. Ask them what they need to think about and then try to close them again."

or they may be saying,

"Ask them how much premium they think they can afford and close them on that."

I can appreciate this strategy has probably worked for you in the past. But it's promoting inadequate cover which I appreciate is the customer's decision and not a noncompliant sale. But just because it's compliant and it has worked in the past, doesn't mean it's truly customer centric. And in my experience, if you're using closing tricks to get people over the line, you're generally experiencing a higher level of policy cancellation.

WRAP UP – SELL THE PROBLEM NOT THE PRODUCT

Wow. That was a lot of work, and I've only shared a few examples of how to use each of these strategies to heighten problem awareness. But as I'll keep telling you throughout this book, if you do the work to help a customer understand and acknowledge the problems their loved ones face, they'll do the work in justifying the premiums and making the decision to purchase adequate cover.

As I mentioned earlier, people will do more to avoid a problem than they will to take advantage of a benefit. But we still need to ensure we effectively sell the benefits of adequate cover and heighten a person's perceived value of adequate cover placed with us and our insurer.

And that's what the next chapter is all about.

CHAPTER FIVE

VALUE EXPECTATIONS – HOW TO PROMOTE VALUE

I trust that what we've covered so far, has given you an understanding that problems are more emotively powerful that benefits. Having said that, if someone has a high level of problem acknowledgement but doesn't perceive you can deliver value, then you have a major problem. That problem is that they're going to go and buy insurance from someone else, despite you doing all the hard work!

Your ability to create a heightened perception of value is a critical skill. Improving your ability to ethically leverage Value Expectation strategies will enable you to increase a prospective customer's perception of the value for money your solutions offer, the value you provide as a guide in their insurance purchasing journey and the importance of buying on value rather than price.

Before we go to the strategies and examples, I want to have a bit of a rant about value proposition and how this concept is failing the financial services industry in general.

THE PROBLEM WITH VALUE PROPOSITIONS

There is value in defining your value proposition, but too many consulting firms, internal training teams and well-meaning sales managers have hacked the concept of value proposition to pieces. There's generally more focus on running a workshop than on how the outputs will be used in the real world of insurance conversations.

Most of you will have experienced what I mean and have probably developed a value proposition like the following...

For the past 45 years, we've served families in the x area by providing holistic advice, focused on helping people understand and manage their risk more effectively, to ensure they and their families live the life they plan on and are protected from an uncertain future.

This is not a bad value proposition. Feel free to cut and paste it onto your website.

Often, I see much worse come out of these styles of workshops. The reason for this is that the person facilitating the workshop refuses to confront the most important aspect of defining and developing a value proposition that will speak to the target market, make it easier for them to choose you and help them differentiate you from the thousands of other agents and options out there. That aspect is,

"What's genuinely different about you, the way you engage your target market in their purchasing journey and the way you create and deliver solutions?"

I would prefer to see something like…

The price you pay for your insurance will depend upon the risk your insurer believes they are taking. We're willing to put the hard work in before we get paid. We're smarter at analysing your risk profile and committed to assisting you in presenting the best possible case to your insurer so that you pay a fair price.

OR

If you're avoiding the insurance discussion, speak to us. We'll make it easy for you to understand what you need and take the "sales" out of helping you buy the right cover.

Call us, and we'll take care of the rest.

OR

We can meet with or speak to you anytime, day or night, to make it easier for you to understand the insurance you really need. We're as passionate about getting you the right solution as we are about making insurance convenient.

OR

There are no dumb questions when you speak to us. Our role is to educate you so that you can make smarter choices and avoid buying the wrong insurance for the wrong reasons. Cheapest is rarely the best value solution. We're all about education and helping you make smarter choices, that protect you and your loved ones, today and into the future.

My big point here is that you need to stop thinking about value as something you say and start thinking about it as something you do. If you can't explain what it is that you "do" differently, the only difference a customer can identify is the price.

Now that my rant is over, let's get back to the reality of insurance sales. With approximately only 5 percent of people telling us they would prefer to buy insurance online, and online dropout rates above 50 percent, none of you are going to get rich by building a website with a great value proposition. Yes – we're back to needing to "do the work" and each of the strategies I'll take you through, require you to work at deliberately heightening the customer's perception of value, throughout the insurance conversation.

STRATEGY #1

BUILDING TOP-OF-MIND AWARENESS OF THE AVAILABILITY OF COVER

We've come a long way, and I'm hoping all of this is motivating you to be more excited about the profession you're in and the opportunities available to you. But it's time to deliver what some of you may consider bad news. And that's the simple fact that no matter how good you are, insurance sales is still a numbers game. You need to speak to a lot of people, a lot of times, over an extended period to be consistently successful in making your sales numbers. You will only ever get out what you put in, but if you use all the strategies I'm sharing you'll get a much better return on your investment.

The primary reason you need to do the numbers is because most people don't wake up each morning thinking,

"I need some more insurance."

We've been through the reasons people don't buy insurance in Chapter 2 so I'm not going to labour this point.

What I am going to labour is the importance of developing skills around turning every opportunity you have into a conversation that makes insurance top of mind for the person you're speaking to. I'll talk about this more when we discuss the Credible Reason step in the ROI Sales Methodology, but let me share a few examples.

When someone asks how are you going instead of saying,

"Not bad,"

or

"I'm hanging in there."

try saying something like the following.

"Great thanks. There's a lot of people out there with the wrong insurance, so that's keeping me nice and busy."

When you're at a networking event, and someone asks you what you do, instead of saying "I sell insurance", say something like the following.

"I'm a specialist in analysing people's risk profiles for their insurance."

You could take this one step further by adding

"That makes it easier for them to negotiate better cover and pricing for their life insurance."

If you're not talking insurance, you can't expect the people you engage with to have the value insurance solutions could deliver them at the top of their mind.

STRATEGY #2

BUILDING CONFIDENCE THAT INSURANCE PAID FOR WILL DELIVER THE COVER REQUIRED SHOULD AN INSURANCE EVENT OCCUR

In a recent survey, I was a little surprised to see that nearly 40 percent of people say that the reason they haven't purchased insurance is because they don't trust insurance companies to make payouts. Recent press in the Australian market certainly hasn't done the industry any favours, and each of us in the industry needs to take personal responsibility for building trust in the insurers we sell for.

I've seen quality assurance checklists that punish salespeople if they fail to talk about how great the insurer they work for is on their telephone calls. While the intent was right; this is a bad strategy because it often forces salespeople to "sell" the insurers credentials to the 60 percent of people that already trust the insurer. When we come across as "trying too hard" to build trust, we do the opposite. I'll touch base on this topic when we consider the Building Rapport and Credibility step in the ROI Sales Methodology, but let me share an important distinction.

The best way to build trust in the insurer you sell for is not to talk about how long they've been in business and how big they are. The best way to build trust is to talk about the claims they have recently paid out to others that were insured. We're back to what you "do", rather than what you say. When you talk about what your insurer is "doing", in relation to paying claims, you provide tangible evidence of the reasons they can and should be trusted.

In my experience insurance salespeople, simply don't spend enough time discussing and interrogating the details of claims paid out by the insurers for whom they sell. This is often a failure on the part of the people that manage them, but that's no excuse for not taking personal responsibility for this as a salesperson committed to being a professional in the industry. Your understanding and ability to tell stories about what claims have been paid out recently is at the core of building trust with those you engage in the insurance conversation. Aligned to this is your ability to talk about claims that weren't paid. This is a problem that generates a lot of interest and makes a thorough analysis and getting the right insurance solution in place significantly more valuable in the mind of the person to whom you're speaking.

STRATEGY #3

DOING THE HARD WORK (UNDERWRITING) WITH THE CUSTOMER TO CONFIRM THEIR ELIGIBILITY FOR COVER AND THE LEVEL OF COVER THEY'RE ABLE TO ACCESS

The psychological Principle of Scarcity tells us that the less available something is and the harder someone must work to get it, the more valuable they will perceive it to be. When discussing the Principle of Consistency and Commitment we explored in the previous chapter, Dr Robert Cialdini notes,

"The evidence is clear that the more effort that goes into a commitment, the greater is its ability to influence the attitudes of the person who made it."[8]

He also notes that as people make small commitments of time and effort, they become significantly more likely to agree to further contributions of time and effort. I'll refer to Cialdini's research throughout this book and strongly recommend you put his books on your reading list.

The way we turn this understanding of human behaviour into practical strategy is first by realising that when a person puts effort into the underwriting process they become more committed to getting a return for that effort by purchasing the available cover. They also become more likely to purchase insurance from the person who put in all that effort.

When you do an initial scan of their eligibility with a couple of basic questions (such as, "Do you smoke?"), and you celebrate them getting past the first eligibility gate, you create a higher perceived value in going through the more detailed process required to confirm eligibility. When you celebrate eligibility, you send a strong message to the person you're engaging with that there is value in their eligibility and that their effort and honesty has been rewarded.

Stop seeing the underwriting process as a hassle and start seeing it as a critical part of your success. Quite simply, the more people you can get to put effort into the underwriting process and the more effort you put into it with them, the more people will buy insurance from you.

STRATEGY #4

GAINING CONFIRMATION THAT THE COST OF PREMIUMS CAN BE PAID FROM THE CUSTOMER'S CURRENT BUDGET

Eligibility is obviously an important gate we need to help a customer through. But even those that are eligible need to think and feel that putting the right amount of cover in place is affordable.

By confirming affordability, we trigger an expectation in the mind of the prospective customer, that not only is there value in the insurance solutions we offer, but also that this value is accessible to them. As I mentioned before, the research is telling us that most people dramatically overestimate how much insurance is going to cost them.

An example of using this strategy within the insurance conversation might go something like this.

SALESPERSON *"OK. From everything we've discussed, the ideal amount of cover to make sure the house is paid out and Mary has three years of household expenses covered would be $650,000. If I use your estimate of $150,000 insurance in your superannuation (group cover in the USA) that leaves a shortfall of about $500,000. Shall I do some numbers on how much that level of cover would cost per month?"*

BILL "Yeah. That makes sense."

SALESPERSON *"Great. I'll put this up to the insurer and get you the fairest price possible. Do you have any thoughts on what the monthly cost is going to be?"*

BILL "I'm not sure."

SALESPERSON *"I just want to make sure we're on the same page so that I don't surprise you when I get the answer back. Just have a guess for me, Bill."*

BILL "I guess around $500 a month?"

SALESPERSON *"I can't guarantee anything Bill but based on your age and health that's probably realistic. If the terms of the policy are right, are you confident you and Mary could make that work in the budget?"*

BILL "I'm not sure."

SALESPERSON *"Thanks, Bill. I'm not after a commitment today. I just want to make sure the numbers I bring you back are going to balance out the need to be covered and the realities of the financial budget. If they can do the $500,000 of cover for around the $500 per month is that something you would seriously consider or is it too far out of the budget?"*

BILL "I think we could fit it in."

SALESPERSON *"Thanks, Bill. Just want to make sure I bring you back a solution that you can put in place. Let's figure out a time for the next meeting. If we can include Mary in that discussion so she can ask any questions directly that would be great. What's the diary like next week?"*

Don't be afraid to have this discussion earlier in the insurance conversation. The more you avoid the money conversation, the more the person you're speaking to will avoid deciding.

Another aspect of this is the legislative requirement to confirm affordability when selling to those in the lower socioeconomic demographic. The legislation is different across states and countries, but affordability conversations are becoming a regulated requirement in many jurisdictions.

My thinking on this is that whether legislation requires you to or not, you need to and should have the affordability conversation in the middle of the insurance conversation, and not at the end as part of a formulaic closing strategy.

STRATEGY #5

BUILDING A SENSE OF RECIPROCITY FOR EDUCATING, ASSISTING AND DELIVERING GREAT SERVICE THROUGHOUT THE INSURANCE PURCHASING JOURNEY

Reciprocity is arguably one of the most challenging English words to pronounce. But, it's also one of the most valuable concepts a salesperson in any industry can incorporate into the way they sell and their life in general. The Principle of Reciprocity tells us that when another person perceives they have received something of value from us, they will feel subconsciously obliged to respond by giving something back. Dr Robert Cialdini suggests there is a "moment of power" when someone acknowledges a favour, and at that point in time people are more likely to return a favour by complying with any reasonable request.

This is an incredibly strong human drive. Think about the people that ended up at your wedding because they invited you to theirs. Think about the friend you helped move because they did the same for you. Think about paying the stranger a few dollars because they cleaned your window at a set of traffic lights even though you tried to wave them off! I'm not saying all of you responded this way, but the research tells us most will.

If we want people to give us their time, their attention, their personal information and a host of other things, the question we need to be asking ourselves is,

"What could I give them first?"

If we want people to give us their business, remain loyal and provide referrals, we need to consider what we could give them throughout the sales process and throughout each year of their cover. The better you get at giving as part of your sales and ongoing customer relationship process, the more likely it is customers will be happy to give you what you need to engage them effectively in the insurance conversation. Let me explain how this concept specifically relates to insurance by sharing a little of my personal experience.

One of the policies I still hold was the first significant ($1m+) policy I put in place approximately 15 years ago when I was in my early thirties. I really like the salesperson that sold it to me. For a long time, I've felt obliged to remain loyal because of all the hard work he did to make sure I took out the right amount of cover.

Early in the process, he took the time to educate me on the different types of insurance cover available and how each could relate to my circumstances and longer-term goals. He and his team made the underwriting process and health checks easy and less confronting. His assistant was highly professional, responsive, always happy to help and proactive in providing great service. The amount of paperwork he had to do to process all the insurance blew my mind, and I really felt like he had to work very hard to turn my needs into cover that was in place. All of this made me think and feel I was receiving real value throughout the insurance conversations we had and the purchasing process we went through. Please note my use of "we" rather than "I".

My point is that he was successful in building a lot of reciprocity (obligation) because he delivered so much value through the way he delivered education, assistance and service as part of the process.

Five years later my business partner was taking care of our personal insurance, to cover a buy/sell agreement in our partnership. I was asked by the salesperson taking care of this insurance if I would like to

"Save some money"

on my other insurance. I flatly said,

"No"

and made the comment that I wanted to acknowledge the other salesperson by remaining loyal because they were the one that got me across the line in putting the right cover in place at a time when I had been putting this off. The salesperson that helped me buy the right cover had delivered so much value through the way they helped me purchase my insurance, that I still felt the obligation to remain loyal.

Dr Robert Cialdini suggests there are three key drivers of reciprocity when we consider the nature of what's given to a person and the amount of reciprocity (obligation) it creates.

The first of those three drivers is the significance (size/dollar value/time value/effort value) of the favour. The bigger the favour, the more reciprocity it is likely to create. So, if you drive out to the airport at 8pm at night to enable a customer to make sure they're insured before they leave on an overseas trip, that's likely to create reciprocity. If you take a client to an expensive game of sport to relationship build, that's likely to create reciprocity.

But there are two challenges with doing significant favours as part of your prospecting and sales process. The first is that those "make or break" opportunities to help the customer out of a bind don't come along in every sale. They don't come along that often at all despite people talking about these moments as if this is the service everyone they sell to experiences. The second problem is that there is generally a very high cost of doing these types of favours. The cost might not just be in dollar terms.

When you drove out to the airport, you probably had to sacrifice a night in with your family and kids.

The good news is that favours don't have to cost a lot to build up the sense of healthy obligation (reciprocity) we wish all our customers felt for us.

The second driver of reciprocity relates to how tailored the favour is. The more a person feels and thinks that the nature of what has been given (the favour) relates to their situation, concerns, likes, dislikes and priorities; the more reciprocity the favour will create. So, if you send them a bottle of wine to say thank you for their business that will generate some reciprocity. If you send them a bottle of Pinot Noir from a wine region they mentioned they want to travel to, and you mention that in the handwritten thank you card, this will create a higher level of reciprocity.

The third driver of reciprocity relates to whether the favour was expected or it was a surprise. The more a favour surprises a person, the greater the level of reciprocity it creates. A bottle of wine given at Christmas with a generic card may create reciprocity. If it was expected and the person doesn't really value wine, it may not create any reciprocity. But if that bottle of wine came six months after they put their policy in place, with a handwritten card saying it was to celebrate your good health, it would be more likely to create a higher level of reciprocity.

Another thing worth mentioning here is that rewards are different to favours. If a person feels like you're doing something for them because you want something back, reciprocity will generally not be created. So, sending the bottle of wine to say,

"Thanks for becoming a customer"

will often be positive, but it's unlikely to increase loyalty or build a subconscious sense of obligation to return the favour at some future time.

I love doing favours. I love sending people books that I've read and loved. I love challenging the way people think and sharing ideas on how they could improve their sales results and have a better quality of life in their sales role. I love entertaining and sharing that with people I do business with and would like to do business with. I really enjoy the free webinars we do and the white papers and other tools we create for our existing and prospective customers. I enjoy spending time with people on a no fee basis to talk about their sales challenges and offering up a few ideas before there's a commercial relationship in place.

And one of the things I love about doing favours as part of my sales process is the way this positively impacts the relationships with the people I do business with. The question you must consider is, what favours are you deliberately doing when you prospect? What favours are built in to the way you engage a person throughout the insurance conversation and what favours do you do each year once they've become a client?

Remember this. If the only thing you do for someone you call a "client" is renew their policy once a year, then you need to be honest about the nature of the relationship. Start calling them a customer.

One other thing I would add to Dr Robert Cialdini's three characteristics of giving for creating reciprocity. Giving only creates reciprocity, where the favour is acknowledged as a favour. If you feel like your hard work is being "taken for granted", it's generally because people don't believe what you're doing is a favour. I'm not suggesting you start using self-serving questions like,

"Did you find that valuable?"

but you do need to be wary of a very common mistake I see and hear salespeople from all industries making.

When a customer says something like,

"Thank you"

or

"That was really useful"

or

"I would never have thought of that"

what they're subconsciously saying is,

"You've provided me with something of value"

This is great. They've given you a signal that at some level you've built reciprocity. But here's where the mistake gets made.

In this "moment of power", instead of saying,

"I'm keen to help you throughout this process"

most of us say something like,

"It's all part of the service"

or

"It wasn't a hassle"

or

"I was driving by anyway"

or some other phrase that suggests it wasn't a favour. In Australia, the most common reciprocity killer is

"No worries"

The problem with these phrases is they literally cancel out any reciprocity that was created!

Worse, they take a person from feeling like they have been treated as an important and special client, to another customer that feels and thinks they're just getting the standard service.

The big point here is that when people acknowledge you for doing a favour, don't kill the reciprocity and at the very least thank them for their acknowledgement.

As I mentioned before, the first salesperson to sell me a significant policy built a lot of reciprocity throughout the insurance conversation and purchasing journey and was rewarded with loyalty five years after the sale was made. But…

As I write this book, I'm currently in the process of reviewing my insurances policies with other providers. It is now 15 years since my current agent put all of my insurance in place. Since then my life has changed completely. My responsibilities to my amazing "wife" (we're not legally married) and beautiful daughter is another huge change. I didn't employ anyone back then, and now the team is 20 people, not including all the consultants that train our system and run their own businesses. My debt profile is radically different, through the investing I've done over the past 15 years. And, as much as I hate to admit it, I'm older!

But here's why I'm not talking to the salesperson whose policy I'm considering replacing. The same salesperson I was raving about a few pages ago! In the past 10 years, I have not received a single proactive call from him. He's delivered no extra value and built no reciprocity through that period, so I feel absolutely no obligation to remain loyal. I know he's still in business because I see him pop up on LinkedIn all the time. If he had called me, I would absolutely have taken his call. But he hasn't, and the lack of reciprocity means I don't feel loyal and to be straight up, I am a little disappointed.

How many of your clients are feeling the way I do?

STRATEGY #6

GAINING A VOLUNTARY AND SPECIFIC COMMITMENT THAT CONFIRMS THE PURCHASE OF INSURANCE IS CONSISTENT WITH THE PERSON'S GOALS/VALUES/ OTHER PURCHASES/ACTIONS

In the previous chapter, we discussed the Principle of Consistency and the power a commitment can have on future behaviour. This includes buying behaviour.

I want to explain how we can ethically leverage commitments made throughout the insurance conversation, to make it more likely that people's behaviour will be consistent with purchasing the right amount of cover. A failure to gain key commitments will often result in people avoiding a decision or taking less cover than their family really needs. To me personally, neither outcome is an option to the truly customer-centric insurance professional.

People don't like to be "told". A classic saying in sales is,

"Stop telling and start selling"

This saying is supported by the research on the power of a voluntary commitment. If you say to someone,

"Something you'll want to cover is the amount of debt on the family home, so I'll give you a quote for that amount of cover. Is that OK?"

most people will say,

"OK"

But the problem you have is they won't feel compelled to include that amount in their insurance solution, because failing to do so, is not inconsistent with anything they've asked for or said. Commitment is only created if they tell you debt on the family home is something they want to cover with their insurance. An example question that would achieve this type of commitment is as follows:

SALESPERSON *"You mentioned debt was something you don't want to leave behind. Is it OK to discuss your current debt levels in a bit more detail?"*

BILL "Sure"

We can then leverage that commitment to have a more detailed conversation to get specific commitments on the amounts of debts the prospective customer may want to cover.

SALESPERSON *"What other debts are there apart from the $250,000 mortgage on the house?*

BILL "There's the credit cards which are about $10,000 and the two cars which are about $40,000."

SALESPERSON *"OK. So, with the mortgage that's a total of about $300,000. How much of that debt would you want your insurance to cover?"*

Let's discuss the value of a specific commitment. You run into an old friend on the street and have a great discussion about old times. If you conclude the discussion with,

"We really should catch up some time"

there's a high probability they will agree. But we all know the probability of doing what it takes to make that happen is very low. On the other hand, if you conclude the discussion with,

"I'm catching up with a few of the old gang this Thursday at 6pm at a bar on 6th Avenue called Flanagan's, would you like to come?"

and they say,

"Yes"

there's a much higher probability they will turn up, even if they've had a hard day at work or really don't feel like a drink. The difference is the level of specificity in the commitment. The more specific a commitment, the more likely people will act consistently with the commitment.

To relate this back to your role as an insurance professional, let's consider two levels of commitment to the amount of insurance a person should take out. If you say,

"Would you like to cover any debt on the house?"

and they say,

"Yes, that would be good"

then you've achieved a commitment. But if you then ask,

"How much is owing on the house?"

and they give you an amount, you've got a more specific commitment. If they give you an answer and you ask,

"Would you want to leave any of that debt behind?"

and they say,

"No"

then you have a much more specific commitment on how much insurance they will need to cover that part of their risk.

The more specific the commitment is, the more likely it is that people will feel subconsciously compelled to behave in a manner that is consistent with that commitment. At the core of The Principle of Consistency is the subconscious desire to be considered a person that behaves in a predictable and consistent manner. Nobody likes an unpredictable person, constantly changing their views and behaving erratically.

And nobody likes to think of themselves as that type of person. Criminals often won't turn on their fellow criminals despite the fact this could reduce their sentence. This is completely irrational, but the core of this lies in the belief that to become a "rat" is inconsistent with their identity of being a criminal.

If someone sees themselves as a good mother, father or partner then doing anything that is not consistent with this feels very uncomfortable. So, if you can get someone to make commitments to the importance of taking care of the family, a lack of funds to support them should something happen, a desire to leave a legacy or anything else that's consistent with taking out the right amount of cover, you increase the probability they will take out the right amount of cover.

Part of being a consistent person includes consistency in your actions. As an example, if you tell your kids that recycling is important, you're more likely to switch off the lights at the office before you leave. If you purchase a security system for the home, you're more likely to spend more money on the locks and other aspects of security in the home. And the classic, if you buy an Apple iPhone, you're more likely to buy a Mac instead of a PC.

So, if you can help someone draw the connection between spending money on school fees because they care about the future of their children, spending money on insurance makes a lot more sense because it feels consistent. If you can help someone draw the connection between insuring the hunk of metal that is their car, spending money on protecting the people they love makes a lot more sense because it feels consistent. And, it feels inconsistent to insure the car and not insure the people they love.

Please remember a point I made above. The key to gaining these sorts of commitments to create this consistency dynamic, by asking questions rather than making statements.

STRATEGY #7

HELPING THE CUSTOMER MAKE A FAVOURABLE COMPARISON WITH ALTERNATIVE OPTIONS/OTHER PURCHASES AND EXPENSES

I have a belief that most people would put the right amount of cover in place if they believed the cost was justifiable.

Something you can do to make the cost more justifiable is help people make more-effective comparisons. Any of you that have parented a teenage daughter will understand this influence strategy. When your partner lets them go to the movies with friends, they'll justify it by saying something like,

"Well, at least she's not at a party with a bunch of 17-year-old boys."

This comparison makes the movies look like a major win! You are a victim to it every time you change over your car. You justify buying a new car, when you don't really need one, by telling yourself something like,

"The monthly payments are pretty much the same."

Your focus on comparing monthly payments removes a consideration of whether you really need a new car and it gives you a great justification.

The more we can help a customer make favourable comparisons like these the easier it becomes for them to justify the cost of insurance. When a customer says something like,

"$200 a month is a lot easier to deal with than thinking about leaving behind $400,000 worth of debts"

you know you've done a great job of enabling them to make a favourable comparison. Let me give an example of how you might set up a favourable comparison.

SALESPERSON *"Mary, you mentioned before that the two children are at Trinity Catholic School. Is that expensive?"*

MARY "It's not too bad. About $2,000 a semester which is a lot cheaper than most private girls' schools."

SALESPERSON *"Great. And are the teachers good over there?"*

MARY "Yeah. I spend a bit of time over at the school, and they're great."

SALESPERSON *"Is there any reason you don't just send them to the local school and save the fees?"*

MARY "I think the school they go to is really important. They get better teaching, and it's a lot safer than the local school."

SALESPERSON *"Understand completely. Safety is a big concern. A lot of the parents I talk to feel the same way, and it sounds like you're getting good value for your money. And are fees for schooling something you would want to cover with the insurance you take out?"*

And later in the insurance conversation...

SALESPERSON *"Mary, from the conversations we've had a lot of this is about protecting Joan and Jenny's future. The good news is that you're eligible for $350,000 of* *cover and that would mean you can make sure the girls have the house with no debt and have their school fees and all other living expenses covered for the next five years. The monthly cost is going to be $289 per month, and I can get that in place today." (Pause and be quiet)*

MARY "That's a little more than I expected. I'm not really sure."

SALESPERSON *"I can appreciate that has to be budgeted for, but I guess if you compare it to what you pay in school fees it's a reasonable price to pay to protect the girls' future. Other than monthly premiums, are there any other concerns with the solution we're discussing?"*

As you can see from the above, this passage of the insurance conversation involved gaining a commitment from Mary around the importance and value of her girls' future. It also created a comparison point the salesperson could ethically use, later in the conversation, if Mary was mentally or emotionally challenged around justifying the cost of the cover.

STRATEGY #8

DEVELOPING A PERSONAL COMMITMENT FROM THE CUSTOMER TO THE VALUE OF THEIR RELATIONSHIP WITH THE SALESPERSON

Let me ask you a very serious question. How likeable are you?

More importantly, how likeable would the last 10 people you've engaged in the insurance conversation with say you are?

Please – take some time out to seriously reflect on this question as it will have a significant bearing on your success as an insurance professional.

I'm not talking about being everyone's best friend here. I'm talking about the science of "liking" and the impact this has on people's behaviour. Liking between two people involves a sense of interdependence. Subconsciously when you're in a state of liking with another person, you're telling yourself,

"This person has my back and I should reciprocate by having theirs."

This mental state is built on the belief that the other person will put your interests ahead of their own personal interests to do the right thing.

The benefits of creating a state of liking between you and a customer or potential purchaser of insurance are significant. People in a state of liking are more likely to agree with each other, more likely to share information, more likely to support each other's recommendations and less likely to do anything that would harm the other person. Once again, reflect on the current state of your relationships and consider whether this accurately describes most your relationships?

I'll talk about more of this in a little more detail in Chapter 9, but for now, let me get you to consider a few of the drivers of liking between two humans. The first driver is the perceived level of similarity between two people. The more a customer feels you are striving for similar goals together, speaking the same language and caring about the same things, the more likely it is there will be a high level of liking. The second driver is the quantity and quality of the exchange between two people. Exchange is fundamentally interaction, and this means the higher the quality of interactions (think conversations) and the greater the quantity of interactions (think – I've been happy to engage in multiple conversations) the more liking there will be. Every-thing I've been sharing with you is aimed at improving the quality of exchange between you and the people with whom you engage in the insurance conversation. Praise is also a driver of liking, and where it's used sincerely it can be a powerful strategy. And the fourth driver of liking is the level of mutual admiration. The more a person admires you, your passion for helping others, your knowledge and process for helping them make better decisions and your focus on helping them to buy, the more they will be in a state of liking with you. Interestingly the more you like and admire them, the more they will like you.

The more effective you are at creating this dynamic in your insurance conversations, the more people will make a personal commitment to the value of their relationship with you. Unfor-tunately, you can only sell insurance to your Mum once, so you need to work on these skills becoming part of your habits and who you are as a person.

If you don't really like people, this is not the industry for you.

STRATEGY #9

GAINING A VOLUNTARY COMMITMENT THAT THE COST OF PREMIUMS IS OUTWEIGHED BY THE VALUE OF BEING FULLY COVERED

When you say something out loud to another person, your com-mitment to what you've said changes dramatically. Last year I decided to run the New York Marathon. I have a busy schedule, and this felt like a big commitment at the time I made it to a friend that I was sharing a drink with. I knew I could weasel my way out of it by avoiding that friend or claiming it was the alcohol speaking, but in my heart I really wanted to tackle this challenge.

The solution? I just told everyone I knew that,

"I'm doing the New York Marathon this November."

On the mornings that I didn't want to run, felt tired, felt like I should work instead of exercise, all I had to think about was facing all those people I'd told about my intention and letting them know I hadn't done the training. As you've read, the level of inconsistency that failing to train would have created, made me feel extremely uncomfortable because I had made a very public commitment. And it was that discomfort that got me out of bed most mornings and kept me on the road for longer and more painful distances than I was used to.

If you can get a prospective customer to tell you out loud that covering their family's future is worth missing out on a dinner out once a month, they become significantly more likely to behave in a manner that's consistent with that commitment. If you gain this commitment out loud before you ask them to proceed with the cover, most people will close themselves.

The favourable comparisons strategy we've already discussed often promotes people making this commitment out loud. An example of how you could ethically use questions to get this level of commitment and Value Expectation would go something like this.

SALESPERSON *"Mary, you mentioned that you're paying $2,000 per semester for the girls' schooling and that you felt this was good value for money when you compared the schooling they would get at the local free school. So, if we compare the $8,000 a year you spend on school for the girls each year, does a premium of $2,400 a year to get all the cover we've discussed make sense?"*

STRATEGY #10

GUIDING THE CUSTOMER TO MENTALLY AND EMOTIONALLY EXPERIENCE THE PEACE OF MIND THAT HAVING THEIR INSURANCE AFFAIRS IN ORDER WILL DELIVER

There's very little difference between vividly imagining something happen, and it happening in real life. The emotional responses in the body are very similar. It's these emotional responses that drive our actions and the urgency of those actions. So, if you can help someone vividly experience what it would be like to have the right cover in place, you make it more likely they will become emotional about putting it in place.

Here's where we hit a few hurdles. The first hurdle is that most people don't want to vividly imagine their own death. And, most of us don't really feel that comfortable asking,

"What would your family's life be like if you died tomorrow?"

The second hurdle is that insurance is one of the few products in the world that offers no immediate and tangible benefit. When I buy a beer at the local pub I get to watch it getting poured, I get to feel that chilled glass as I pick it up, I get to cheer the mates I'm drinking it with, I get to drink down that first frothy sip and let out a big happy sigh as I swallow it down. Anyone feel like a beer? For the beer drinkers, out there, notice that I sold you on the value of beer, without talking price. All I had to do was take you to that place where you experience all the benefits in your mind.

But when I think about signing the insurance papers, there's not a raft of emotional thoughts that naturally buzz through my brain causing me to feel a sense of joy and value. The key to creating an emotional response is to ethically help people experience the downside of not having cover in place. We can make something seem much sweeter by contrasting (comparing) it to something bitter.

An example of how you might do this ethically would be a questioning string like this:

SALESPERSON *"Bill, it's not the most comfortable conversation but have you had a friend that's passed away or suffered something like a heart attack or cancer?"*

BILL "Yeah. A good friend of my daughter lost her father recently. I didn't know him but that's what prompted my enquiry."

SALESPERSON *"Understand completely. It's a lot easier to talk to someone before this stuff happens than talking to their family after it has happened. Do you know if they had enough insurance in place to cover off everything we've discussed about debts, living expenses and leaving a legacy?"*

BILL "I'm not really sure?"

SALESPERSON *"Let me ask you a question. If I could send you back in time and you could make sure they did have the right insurance in place, would you do it?"*

BILL "Obviously, that would be great."

SALESPERSON *"It would be great. And I would love to be able to do that for their family. But unfortunately, I can't go back in time and neither can you. How would you be feeling right now if that was your family and you had passed away without putting the insurance we're talking about in place?"*

I can understand this might be a little too challenging for several of you. This sort of conversation requires courage and if you're just using it as a scare tactic, it will come across poorly to the person you're speaking to. Having this sort of conversation requires integrity, empathy and a genuine care for the people you sell to. The big point I'm making in relation to this strategy is that the more a person has vividly experienced value in their mind the higher their Value Expectation will be.

WRAP UP – INCREASING THE FOCUS ON VALUE REDUCES THE FOCUS ON PRICE

As we discussed in the previous chapter, the primary driver of any insurance purchase is likely to be a desire to solve a problem that has been acknowledged. Having said that, the more a person expects to achieve value, the easier it is for them to justify the cost of insurance.

The PAVE Principle tells us that the more people acknowledge the problems associated with a lack of cover the more likely it is they will purchase the right amount of cover. It also tells us that the more they experience value through your guidance and expect value through the purchase the more likely it becomes they will purchase insurance from you.

Now that we understand the psychology behind the insurance purchasing decision making, let's move on to applying this understanding inside a sales process that will set you up for success.

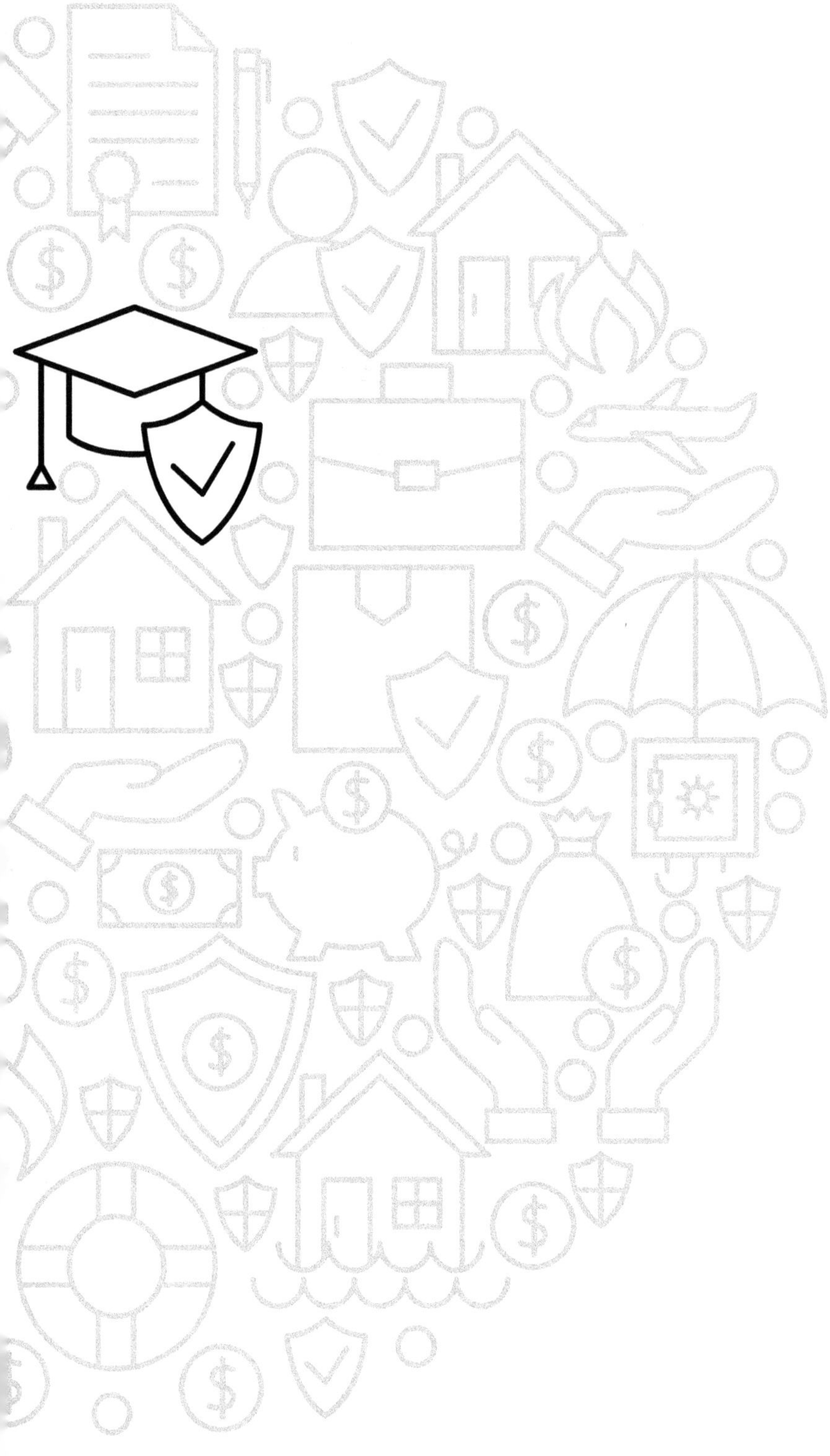

CHAPTER SIX

UNDERSTANDING AND ADOPTING THE ROI SALES METHODOLOGY

WHY ADOPT A SALES METHODOLOGY?

The way you sell, can and should give you a competitive advantage.

It should make people want to place their cover through you. It should decrease the likelihood that they'll shop around for price. And it should enable you to achieve higher premium sales, because it ethically causes people to place more emphasis on the risk in their lives than the cost of insuring them.

Most sales methodologies are the same, and none give you a competitive advantage. Competitive advantage comes from the way you put your methodology into practice and the way your leader and peers coach and motivate your continuous improvement. A clearly defined sales methodology enables you to become aware of what works – capture it and repeat it.

Whether you adopt the ROI Sales Methodology or another, the most important thing is that you have one. Your methodology is a written description of the process you need to take a customer through, for them to decide on whether they buy your product or not. The more everyone in your organisation agrees on this process, the more alignment there will be between the reality of your sales role and support from leaders, coaches, marketing and other important functions within your business. I'll use the terms "sales methodology" and "sales process" interchangeably throughout the rest of this book.

That's why the ROI Sales Methodology is open source. If you attribute it to SalesITV (the sales performance consulting company I co-founded), you're welcome to use it inside your organisation or personally. You can even access free video content, training the methodology at www.salesroi.com

Adopting a sales methodology is all about developing an awareness of the customer's insurance purchasing journey. This is the journey you need to guide a customer through to help them buy the right cover for their situation. The more aware you are of where a customer is on the journey, the more effective you'll be as their guide.

What I mean by "awareness" is developing a conscious approach. Being aware that at each step of the customer's purchasing journey, they need you to deliver on different rational and emotional needs. The ROI Sales Methodology enables you to understand and deliver on these rational and emotional needs at each step of the customer's journey.

As the customer's guide, your ability to move the customer forward on their journey will be defined by your ability to engage them in an insurance conversation. Throughout this book, I've used the terms "insurance journey", "insurance purchasing journey" and "insurance conversation" interchangeably. I hope it has been clear that they all refer to the way you engage the person you're helping buy the right insurance cover.

If you're self-centred and focused on selling something, people are significantly less likely to want you to assist them with their insurance purchasing journey. People are more likely to respond favourably and partner with you on their insurance journey if you're focused on helping them understand their risk(s) and buying the right cover. The more you develop your skills in each step of the methodology, the better you'll get at meeting the customer's needs and maintaining engagement. As most of you know, these can be long journeys and your ability to maintain engagement is critical to your success and the wellbeing of those to whom you sell.

All of this means you need to adopt a defined methodology. The clearer you are about what you're doing and why you're doing it, the more successful (and compliant) your insurance conversations will be.

Think about this for a moment. Ask yourself whether you can confidently draw your current sales methodology. You might also call this a sales process. Take a little time out to draw it on a piece of paper and define what the customer's rational and emotional needs are at each stage or step. Please challenge yourself to do this exercise on paper. If you're a CEO telling yourself,

"We've already rolled out a training session on sales"

I challenge you to test whether your front line can do this exercise. Hit the floor and separately ask four of your salespeople to whiteboard the trained process and how they meet customer's rational and emotional needs at each step or stage.

WHAT'S
THE ROI ABOUT?

Let me explain why our sales process is called the ROI Sales Methodology.

We call our sales process the ROI Sales Methodology to remind you that when you're in a sales situation, you need to achieve three things:

First – You need to make sure that the customers and prospects you engage with are getting a return on the time, effort and money they spend with you. The more you focus on ensuring customers achieve value, the easier it is to make sales. The less you sell and the more you help people buy, the more value they'll experience on their insurance purchasing journey.

Second – You need to make sure that the price at which you sell products or services at achieves a return for the company for which you work. Sales is not about giving customers everything they want at the lowest price possible. All of us need to remember that without profit, your company, your job and your ability to provide customers with great service and solutions – doesn't exist. The more customer centric your approach, the less exposed you are to losing business to price-focused competitors.

And third – You need to make sure that you're achieving a return on the time and effort you put into helping customers and prospects buy the right solution. There is always enough time to achieve your sales targets if you're not wasting time on customers that aren't prepared to pay a fair price, don't want what you sell or just aren't ready to buy. Selling insurance is a numbers game but the higher the quality of your insurance conversations, the lower the quantity of conversations you'll require to be successful.

Being a sales professional is all about developing the sales skills, behaviours and beliefs that support achieving the best return on investment possible for everyone involved in the sale.

Let's go through each of the steps in the ROI Sales Methodology at a high level. In the chapters that follow I'll take you through more detail on how to execute each of these steps.

WHERE DO WE START?

When I ask,

"What's the first step in any good sales process or methodology?"

there's always a variety of answers relating to things like building rapport, product knowledge, targeting the right customers, researching and needs analysis. These are important aspects of any process, but I challenge the notion that this is where you begin.

We begin with the number one driver of success – you and what's going on in your head!

OUTCOME FOCUS

The first step in any great sales methodology is ensuring that you're mentally set up to succeed.

What's critical in this step is developing clarity around the outcomes you need to achieve before you pick up the phone, go to a meeting and even write an email. This step is about maximising your productivity and getting the most out of every customer interaction throughout the journey.

Remember – if the only outcome in your head is,

"Selling something"

the response in the customer's heart and mind is likely to be a desire to avoid talking to you.

HAVE A
CREDIBLE REASON

If you sell insurance from a call centre environment, you've probably experienced quite a few days where getting on the phone to call relative strangers was incredibly difficult. You're probably also experiencing quite a low rate of call to engagement, and in my experience, this is often as low as 3–5% of every 100 outbound dials. This tells you the people you're calling are not motivated to speak to an insurance salesperson.

If you're an advisor, you might not make 100 calls a day, but for most of you, an honest review of your portfolio of clients will show that insurance uptake vs. potential insurance uptake is low. A review of the CRM will probably also show that you're not making enough outbound calls and if you track it, your call to engagement rate is also lower than desired.

Why is this? Australia is one of the most underinsured nations in the world and in the US only three out of 10 Americans believe they have enough insurance. Surely people would want to take your call?

The core of the problem is a failure to develop and effectively communicate what I call a "credible reason" for engagement. This needs to be focused on something the prospective customer cares about. It must trigger an acknowledgement in the person engaged that your call is likely to deliver them value for their time and any information you might ask them for.

You will achieve an amazing return on your effort if the only skill you develop by reading and applying what you learn in the book is the ability to develop and deliver a credible reason. We'll get to that in Chapter 8.

BUILD RAPPORT AND CREDIBILITY

If you sell insurance in a call centre your ability to rapidly generate a sense of trust between you and the person you're speaking to is critical. Trust is conversational oxygen, and without it you simply won't be able to maintain engagement without resorting to pushy, self-centred communication strategies that destroy customer experience.

For a person to trust you commercially, they need to feel both comfortable and confident in the conversation.

Their level of comfort will be defined by your ability to rapidly develop rapport and avoid common communication mistakes that break the emotional connection between you and the customer. Building rapport should be an active, deliberate and planned part of every common communication you have with your prospective customers. Most people who think they're great at winging this, are challenged when we review their calls and show them how many times they broke rapport or failed to take advantage of rapport building opportunities.

Even if you are great at this, rapport on its own is not enough. I'm sure you have many friends and family that are not insured through you.

You must also create confidence by building the perception that your expertise and ethics make you a credible partner for their insurance purchasing journey. Once again there are common mistakes we observe when we review calls. Unfortunately, these mistakes are generally missed in call reviews and coaching. People are more likely to value conversations with people they perceive are experts, and your ability to conduct the insurance conversation in a professional manner is critical in creating this dynamic. And the answer is yes – you can absolutely create the perception that you're an expert without providing personal advice.

I'll take you through several critical trust building strategies you need to be employing, and highlight some of the most common mistakes you want to avoid in Chapter 9.

EXPLORING
AND LISTENING

Effective needs analysis is at the core of creating a customer-centric experience. And empowering, skilling and coaching salespeople to guide a person's insurance journey with great questioning and listening techniques is the key to delivering experiences customers will rave about. When people are guided by great questions, they experience value. And that value translates into lower price sensitivity, less price shopping and lower cancellation rates.

Unfortunately, truly great needs analysis skills are the exception rather than the norm across the industry. There are several reasons for this, including quality assurance processes that punish salespeople for "going off script" and limit the ability of salespeople to truly educate customers with questions. I've come across compliance teams that have argued that a question could be deemed advice. This is nonsense.

If you're the CEO of an insurance company, you need to know what limitations are being put on your front line that put fear above customer needs and experience. Aligned to this is the ability to genuinely listen. Most CEOs and senior leaders that we've worked with have been literally horrified at how a lack of listening skills and strategy translates into poor customer experiences. Listening is arguably the skill that is most deficient across the industry in both phone and field based salespeople.

If you're a salesperson your greatest strength should be your ability to ask the right questions, listen with empathy and guide a conversation by asking questions rather than making statements. In Chapter 10, I'll teach you how to do that without giving advice. If you're able to give personal advice, these skills will still be incredibly valuable.

The person that feels like they chose to buy, is much more likely to become a customer than the person who feels like they were told what to do.

GAINING PERMISSION

A customer needs to make a series of decisions as they progress through the steps in their insurance journey. The more effective you are at seeking a person's permission to move to the next step in the insurance conversation, the more it becomes their journey rather than your sale.

You also need to gain the permission of your employer/insurer to provide the cover people need and ideally want. The underwriting process is a critical part of the journey that very few customers understand or enjoy.

Throughout the entire book, I'll teach you how to ethically build customer commitment. This is the key to productivity, generating higher returns on your efforts and ensuring people make decisions to put the right cover in place. In Chapter 11, I'll give you tips and strategies for being more effective in the underwriting phase of the journey.

OFFERING SOLUTIONS

If you've done the work, presenting a solution should be more about confirming what the customer has told you than pitching the value of insurance. This is the key to selling without providing personal advice. And once again, even if you can provide advice, this is the key to making the customer feel like they're buying rather than being sold to.

I'll give you strategies for presenting the solution back to the customer, which will enable you to deliver an ethically persuasive confirmation of needs and a compliant solution presentation. This is a critical moment in the customer's journey and seamlessly moving between the presentation of solutions, underwriting, administrative requests (like payment details) and customer concerns is a critical skill you must develop.

ASKING FOR OUTCOMES

The final "close" in an insurance conversation should be a confirmation rather than a close. The only thing you should be closing at this stage is a confirmation that the customer wants to place their cover with you and the insurer you represent.

I call this step "asking for outcomes" because I like to make the point that a great insurance conversation generally involves more than one call. If you have great CRM data, it is highly likely you'll notice a strong correlation between the number of customer conversations and the cancellation rate. The single call sale is far more likely to result in cancellation than the multi-call purchasing journey.

The very best insurance salespeople are asking for the customer to commit to making decisions throughout the entire journey. They know what their outcomes are for each stage of the journey and they confirm these have been achieved before moving forward. I'll highlight the key moments in the journey where you need to be asking for outcomes and decisions and share strategies for achieving closes in an ethical and customer-centric manner.

HANDLING OBJECTIONS

I've labelled this step in the ROI Sales Methodology "handling objections" because that's the common language used to describe anything that causes a customer not to buy. My personal preference in language is to refer to objections as "concerns".

If you've done the work, the person you're speaking to will have educated themselves on their need for insurance cover. They will have confirmed out loud that they have that need. You will have helped them quantify that need through great questioning and listening. So, if the person you're speaking to is reluctant to move forward on the purchasing journey, they're signalling a concern rather than an objection. The more you react to objections as concerns, the more customer centric you become in handling them.

If they don't have a need, you shouldn't be getting any objections because you shouldn't be trying to sell them insurance!

In Chapter 14 I'll provide you with strategies to comfortably and confidently engage customers around their concerns. Importantly, I'll show you how to do this in a way that enables the customer to overcome their concern, rather than putting the pressure on you to overcome their objection.

NEXT STEPS

Statistically, many of the people you call or speak to will experience an insurance event in their lives. As an example, our office on the 6th and 7th floors experienced "a flood" when an air conditioner pipe exploded over Easter! I'm rather thankful our insurance salesperson sold us cover that included insuring us for water damage.

But we were covered for our unexpected insurance event. And most aren't. The sad thing about this is how many of them spoke to an insurance salesperson before the event, confirmed they had a need and then failed to purchase insurance. As a truly customer-centric salesperson you must commit to follow up. As I mentioned earlier, success and longer-term commitment from customers generally requires multiple calls with a customer, before they put the right cover in place or truly decide to keep paying for the cover they've purchased. In Chapter 15 I'll share the strategies used by the best salespeople to maintain engagement over multiple calls. This may seem like a small distinction, but there are over 10 specific strategies the top performers include at the end of calls, that the poor performers don't.

TOO COMPLICATED?

I'm often told that nine steps or stages is too complicated for the average insurance salesperson. There's desire to simplify sales process down to four or five steps to make it easier to remember and easier to coach. At SalesITV, we have a five-step sales process we could sell customers with this concern. But we challenge whether this is in the customer's interests and do our best to sell our customers what they need rather than what they want. There are two major reasons, all nine steps in the process, should be adopted by insurance salespeople. This is the case, whether they sell on the phone or face to face and whether they can provide personal advice or not.

The first is that in my experience insurance salespeople tend to be significantly more intelligent than their leaders give them credit for. If you treat and train people in dumb ways, you tend to get dumb behaviour in response to this.

The second reason I suggest using the nine-step approach, is the importance of each of the steps. If your skill level is poor in relation to any one of the nine steps the overall quality of a customer interaction is likely to be poor. Each step represents a critical skill set that must be coached and developed. If you miss a step you decrease the probability of purchase.

I can bundle the nine sets of skills into a 4- or 5-step model, but that doesn't change the fact that you need to be good at all of them to consistently achieve 100% compliance, great customer experiences and great sales results. In our experience, breaking the sales process into these nine steps makes it easier to train, observe, reflect on and coach each step.

COMMIT TO CUSTOMER-CENTRIC SALES BEHAVIOURS

The rest of this book is all about making sure the way you sell supports customers thinking and feeling like they're buying. If you adopt the ROI Sales Methodology and commit to mastering it and following it, you will dramatically fast-track your success. Importantly, adopting a clearly defined process and following it is also the best way to ensure the success of the customers you serve and compliance in the way you sell.

Committing to the customer-centric way includes committing to excellence in the way you help people buy insurance.

In the following chapters, we'll consider each step of the ROI Sales Methodology and how to apply it to the insurance conversations critical to your success.

CHAPTER SEVEN

OUTCOME FOCUS

WHAT'S OUTCOME FOCUS ALL ABOUT?

Do you consistently feel highly productive or are most of your days busy, challenging and overwhelming?

At the core of the ROI Sales Methodology is outcome focus. This is to remind you that the first thing you need to consider before you act, is the outcomes you're trying to achieve through your efforts. This applies whether you're about to write an email, make a phone call, go to a meeting, present a solution and even head off to a social event. Productive and successful people do not have more time in their day than you do. They just use their time more effectively. Something that was pointed out to me early in my career was that lost money could be recouped, but lost time was gone forever.

Being outcome focused is about making conscious decisions on what you want to achieve and smarter choices about how you achieve those outcomes. It's about adopting a more disciplined approach to constantly improving your ability to achieve the outcomes that drive success for you, your customers and the company you work for.

GAINING CLARITY ON OUTCOMES

I think the best way to explain the value of this concept is to share an example of a very smart client of mine in Hong Kong that was behaving in a very dumb way.

It was 3.30pm in the afternoon, and we were driving towards some specific actions following an exhausting day of strategy facilitation.

One of the key people came up to me in the break before we were about to head back in and said they needed to leave to make some urgent phone calls. I asked them what the urgency was and the interaction went like this...

SMART CLIENT *"I've had a couple of clients pull out of the Phil Collins concert tonight, and I need to do a ring around of other clients to see who can make it along."*

ME "OK. What outcome are you trying to achieve out of taking clients to the concert?"

SMART CLIENT *"What do you mean?"*

ME "You're spending money and time taking people to this concert, and I'm assuming you'll be away from your family tonight. What do you want to achieve for this investment?"

SMART CLIENT *"It's a relationship thing."*

ME "OK. So your outcome is to build a better relationship with the people you're taking along, right?"

SMART CLIENT *"Yes."*

ME "So, if someone rang you up three hours before a concert and said, someone else has dropped out, do you want to come to the concert, do you think that sends a message that they're an important relationship for you?"

SMART CLIENT *"I guess not, but I don't want to waste the tickets."*

ME "I get that. But how could you utilise the tickets <u>and</u> build a relationship? Do you have other clients coming along?"

SMART CLIENT *"Yes."*

ME "What if you rang those clients and said you've had a last-minute cancellation and thought they might want to bring someone else from their office or a friend or partner. Do you think that would be a good relationship builder?"

SMART CLIENT *"OK, I get it. I'll make that call and be back in the room in 5."*

The reason this is such an important and powerful strategy is that most of us are so busy doing "stuff" and responding to urgency, that we lose sight of what we're trying to achieve. The clearer you are about the outcome, the more likely it is you'll be smart about achieving it. The vaguer the outcome, the more likely it is your effort is not going to achieve what really matters.

Another great example of how easy it is to lose sight of what you're really trying to achieve is when salespeople spend hours trying to craft the perfect relationship-building email. If you want to build a relationship pick up the phone! Or even better, go out and see the person.

Before you act, stop and ask yourself,

"What am I actually trying to achieve with the effort I'm about to use?"

BETTER STRATEGIES AND ADDITIONAL OUTCOMES – THE KEY TO PRODUCTIVITY

Let's apply this to a common challenge for most insurance sales-people. The dreaded networking event! Before I give you some guidance, take a little time out to consider how you think the concept of outcome focus might make you smarter and more productive in relation to attending a networking event.

Seriously – just take a little time out to do some thinking on this.

Let's start with

"What am I actually trying to achieve with the effort I'm about to use?"

If you really stop and think about this, you'll realise that your primary outcome for attending a networking event should be to build your network of people that are open to engaging with you in an insurance conversation. You'll realise that you need to set some targets for things like the number of new people you meet, the number of people you get details from and the number of people that verbally confirm they would be happy to meet with you. Just taking some time out to do this will make you significantly smarter in your approach. It will also increase the probability a return will be achieved, on the time and money you invest in going to the event.

When you remind yourself the goal is to meet new people, you might get a little smarter and turn up early for the event. This is when people are most likely to be on their own and most open to meeting someone who says,

"Hi. The person I'm meeting here hasn't arrived yet either. How did you get invited along?"

This is likely to result in you meeting them and the person they planned to meet. It means there are two of you and that will make it easier to introduce yourselves to anyone else who turns up early and is on their own. Smart outcomes lead to smarter strategies, and that leads to better results.

But what if you were also smart enough to ask,

"What other outcomes can I achieve?"

If you asked this question enough, you might realise one of your prospective or existing customers would get value out of the event. You could ring them and ask if they would like to buddy up with you for the event and do some joint networking. Even if they can't make it, this will still generate additional perceived value in the relationship with you. You might also realise that you could ask a third-party referrer (like an accountant who sends you people to talk to) along to the event. This would give you a chance to build that relationship and make it more likely they will refer more often.

In this one example, just asking smarter questions about outcomes will enable you to achieve significantly higher returns, with very little extra effort. That's at the core of this strategy and why it's at the core of the ROI Sales Methodology.

FIRST MEETINGS – CRITICAL OUTCOMES

In the insurance industry, meetings with prospective customers are valuable.

To honour that value and achieve better ROI, you need to be deliberate and strategic about the outcomes you should be achieving in a first meeting. There are six critical outcomes (the 6 C's) you need to ethically achieve to make it more likely that a first meeting will lead to the right cover for the person to whom you're speaking.

CRITICAL OUTCOME #1

CONTEXT THAT BUILDS ENGAGEMENT

The way you open the insurance conversation will have a dramatic impact on a person's desire to share information, participate in the process and willingly acknowledge the problems they face if sufficient cover is not in place. When we achieve great context for the meeting, we increase the probability people will actively engage in the insurance conversation they need to have.

Take some time out to think through how you open your first meetings with prospective customers. How effectively are you setting the scene for an open, educational and valuable conversation? How effectively are you communicating the value a person will achieve if they give you their time and details of their personal life? Are you pacing out any objections they might have to reduce the impact these will have on the conversation? Are you setting up a clear framework for the process you want to take them through?

Your ability to frame the context of a meeting will dramatically impact the quality of your conversations and the willingness of prospective customers to engage with you.

CRITICAL OUTCOME #2

COMFORT IN ENGAGING

The insurance conversation is a highly personal discussion that requires the prospective customer to share lots of personal and financial information. The more comfortable a person feels, the more information they will share and the more effective you can be in giving them guidance on how to buy the right insurance cover. This means rapport-building skills and generating a sense of liking with a prospective customer is extremely important.

Take some time out to consider how deliberate and effective you are at building a sense of comfort when you engage prospective customers. What are you doing to build this throughout the insurance conversation? How do you know if what you're doing is working? How deep is your understanding of rapport building and the science of liking that explains how to achieve this comfort in the relationship? How adaptive is your style when dealing with a diverse customer base?

Your ability to achieve comfort early in the conversation will significantly impact the customer's behaviour throughout and following the meeting.

CRITICAL OUTCOME #3

CONFIDENCE IN ENGAGING

Because the insurance conversation requires someone to share a significant amount of information about their financial situation, people need to feel confident about the person with whom they're sharing that information and the company with which they work. If you're not deliberately building this confidence in your credibility, there's a strong chance people will focus significantly more on how much they must spend rather than on how much risk they must cover.

Take some time out to consider how effectively you're positioning yourself as a valuable expert and source of insurance wisdom. Whether you can offer advice or not, what are you deliberately doing to build your perceived credibility when you engage people? Is there anything you're doing that might be damaging this? Are there things you could be doing before the meeting to build this? How do you know people leave a first meeting with you feeling confident you're the ideal partner for the insurance conversations they need to have and the insurance cover they need to put in place?

People are more likely to engage with you, listen to you, value what you have to say and ask and give you their time if they perceive you're an expert they can have confidence in.

CRITICAL OUTCOME #4

CONCERN IN FAILING
TO COVER RISKS

As we explored in the PAVE Principle, people are much more likely to act and get emotional about acting if they acknowledge there is a problem that needs solving. Your role is to ethically create that concern where there is a risk in a person's life, that they and their loved ones are not covered for. If you leave a first meeting where there is a genuine need for cover, and you have not created a level of concern, you've failed. That seems harsh, but this failure is what causes people to not cover risks, and that's what leads to families going through the financial pain my family went through.

Go back to the PAVE Principle and really get honest with yourself about how effective (and ethical) you are at building concern where there are risks in a person's life that need to be acknowledged and quantified. Are you achieving this state by educating the customer with great questions or are you making too many statements? Are you doing the work to effectively quantify the real risks to make them more real and concerning? Are you covering off all the potential risks or are you rushing to get a dollar amount of the cover desired so you can quote a premium price? When people leave a first meeting with you are they more concerned about their risks or the cost of cover?

Momentum in the sales process is driven by customer concern. Every person you've quoted over the years that failed to decide is a person that left the insurance conversation without enough concern to take action.

CRITICAL OUTCOME #5

CLARITY ON
THE WAY FORWARD

The clearer someone is about the process for achieving the understanding they need and the cover that's required, the more likely it is that they will fully engage in the process. The more clarity they have around why you and the company you work for are the right fit for achieving their insurance needs, the more likely it is they will follow through on purchasing the right cover from you. When you finish the first meeting, this level of clarity needs to be established to make it more likely you'll be their preferred insurance provider.

Think through the last couple of first meetings you've had and consider how much clarity the person you were speaking to left the meeting with. Did they have absolute clarity on the risks that they needed to cover and your ability to help them achieve this? Did they have clarity on why the insurer you recommended or work for was the right partner for them to choose in achieving the cover required? Were they clear on the next steps, what they had to do to put the cover in place and when they would achieve cover if they continued with the process?

Prospective customers with clarity purchase insurance. Great salespeople create that clarity.

CRITICAL OUTCOME #6

COMMITMENT TO ACT

The final outcome is the true test of whether you've effectively engaged someone in a valuable insurance conversation. If you've achieved the first five outcomes people will be more than happy to commit to actions that are consistent with putting the right cover in place.

Go back to several recent conversations that have stalled. Which people have you spoken to that are either not returning your calls, or just avoiding putting into place the cover they need? What level of commitment did you achieve in the last conversation you had with them? What specific commitments did you achieve and were there any commitments you failed to achieve? Do you have a clearly articulated list of the commitments you need to achieve, to make it more likely first meetings will make it more likely customers will act and put the right cover into place?

A committed person is more likely to purchase cover. Great salespeople are deliberate about creating commitments, consistent with purchasing the right cover.

ARE YOU ACHIEVING THE 6 C'S?

I really want you to take some time out to consider all the questions above. In our workshops, we leverage the 6C First Meeting Framework to help insurance salespeople understand the importance of these questions and the how to achieve each of the C's in first meetings. I want to acknowledge that it often takes multiple meetings to achieve all the C's, but as an insurance professional, your goal should be to leave the first meeting with these outcomes achieved.

The PAVE Principle and all the strategies I shared in that part of the book will help you achieve all these outcomes. Application of the ROI Sales Methodology will ensure this happens consistently and that's good for you and the customer.

WRAP UP

Outcome focus is all about making sure you are in the right mental state to achieve higher productivity. This drives a better return on time and effort for you, your customers and the organisation for whom you work. This is the first step in the ROI Sales Methodology, and if you get into the habit of starting with the outcome in mind, you'll consistently achieve a smarter approach to the way you use your valuable time, energy and effort.

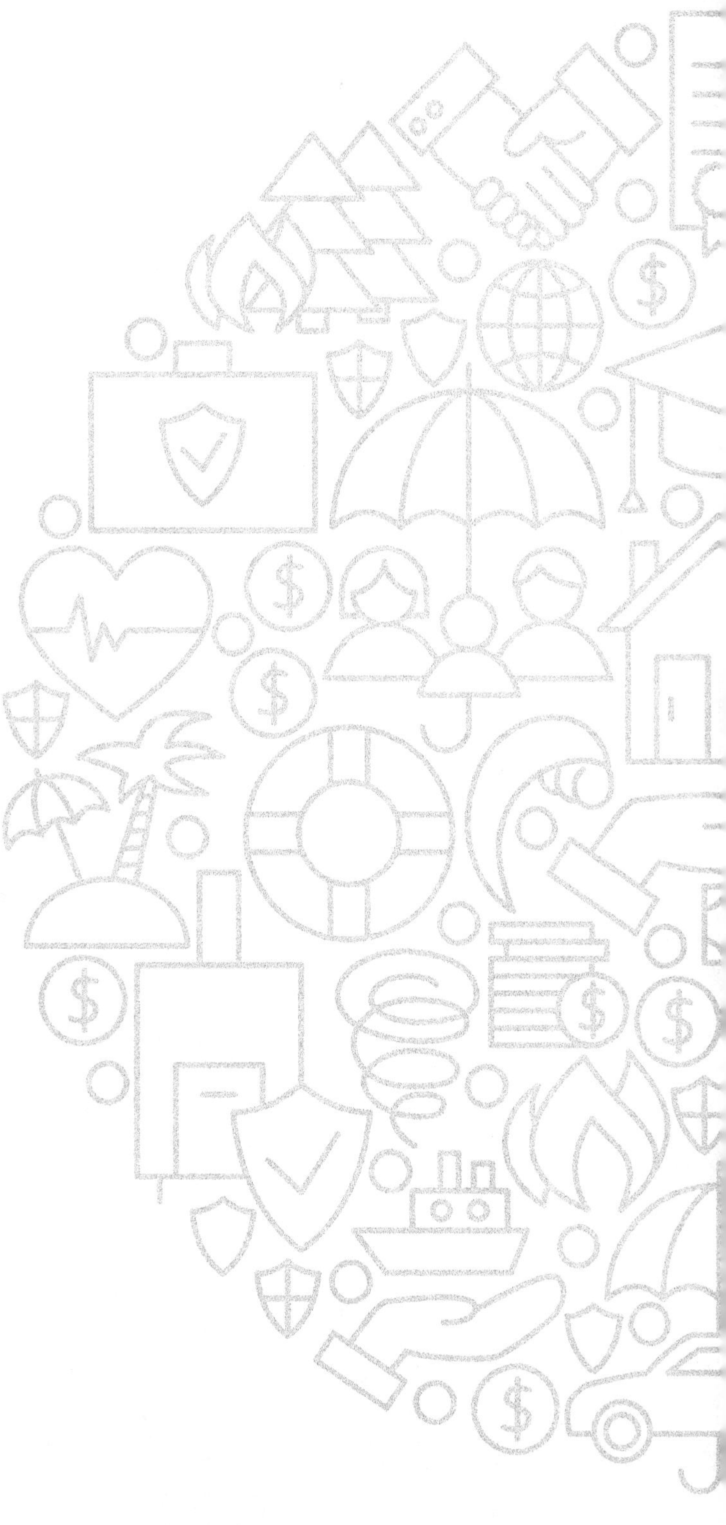

CHAPTER EIGHT

HAVING A CREDIBLE REASON

HOW EFFECTIVE AND EFFICIENT IS YOUR ENGAGEMENT OF "LEADS"?

How easily are you connecting with prospective customers?

This is probably, the most important question an insurance salesperson, their manager and the organisation for whom they work should be considering daily. In the insurance industry, my experience suggests too little time is spent seriously considering this question, in a customer-centric manner.

CEOs and General Managers blinded by historical lead to conversation metrics are accepting what I consider to be a very poor rate of return on the leads generated through marketing expenditure. At a sales leadership and coaching level, too much emphasis is placed on the quantity of outbound activity, and too little on the quality and customer centricity of that activity. And at a salesperson level, too much time is wasted blaming "the leads". Too little time is spent on taking personal responsibility, for developing the skills, mindset and techniques required to increase the likelihood that contact with another person will result in a willingness to engage in the insurance conversation.

Everybody is to blame for the current state of affairs. While selling insurance is a numbers game, salespeople must take responsibility for what they can control and be better in this area.

For those of you not selling insurance from a call centre, you may think that this chapter is not that relevant. I'll talk a lot about using outbound calls to engage prospective customers, and that might not be something you do or think you should be doing. I can understand why you would think that. But I suggest you'll still get a lot of value out of this chapter. This is relevant whether you're trying to secure a meeting with a cold lead or calling someone that's been referred to you. It applies when you're calling an existing customer to suggest a more detailed review of their affairs. It applies when you call someone to invite them to an event or suggesting they engage with another specialist you work with or refer to.

The ability to develop a credible reason is core to the customer-centric way of selling, so please take the time out to read this chapter, reflect on its relevance, and consider adopting this step every time you engage existing and prospective customers.

CUSTOMER CENTRICITY DRIVES CREDIBILITY

Outcome focus was all about you. Taking the time out to consider what outcomes you need to demand and achieve, to get a return on your valuable time, energy and effort. Having a credible reason is about realising that the most effective and efficient manner for achieving your outcomes is aligning those with the outcomes that matter to the people in your target market. The more customer centric your marketing is, the more effective and efficient it will be. Let me explain by sharing what I experienced when I left the law and worked with a property development company.

It was the early '90s and child care in Australia was an industry that was taking off, on the back of changes to government funding. There was a significant and unmet demand from a workforce requiring flexibility and quality care for young children under school age. I was running a property development company, making big moves in the industry and on the target list of a significant number of banks wanting to lend money to developers in this space.

It was crazy. I was managing approvals, construction and operating centres across a 250km territory and working insanely long days and nights. Cash flow was a constant challenge, not just because of capital outlays, but also because of the number of parent payments involved in running each centre. Accounting in the industry had not yet evolved to make it easy to collect cash from parents, reconcile this with government funding, and report in a manner that ensured balance payments from the government were received in a timely manner. To say I had my hands full would have been a major understatement.

I would constantly get calls from bankers explaining what bank they were from, their title at the bank, and suggesting that I should meet with them. The reason for the meeting they would offer was generally something like this,

"I would like to meet with you to tell you about the bank and find out more about your business."

Before I explain why this was not well received, I want you to pause for a moment and think about this statement from a customer-centric point of view. One of the things you need to understand about a customer-centric approach is what motivates customers must be central to the way you engage. Prospective customers (and existing customers) don't really care about your interests until they know you care about theirs. So, any statement that is primarily focused on your interests is not likely to be well received by a person with whom you don't have a current relationship.

"Find out more about (my) business" offered no clear value to me, the prospective customer. Knowing more about the bank that was trying to sell me something, offered even less. When I would hear this reason for calling I would always think to myself,

"Why don't you do some research on my company and then come out and tell me how you can help me better than any other bank in the market!"

Needless to say, no banker was ever successful at securing a meeting with this bank/salesperson-centric approach. If someone had used a more customer-centric approach, like the following, they would have been successful in securing my time and attention.

"Several of our other child care customers have been telling us a major challenge for them revolves around accounting for parent payments and the cash flow gap between getting paid by the parents and getting paid balances from the government.

We did some research on what the best child care centres are doing to collect money more

effectively and what the best accounting practices are in the industry.

I was hoping to spend some time to take you through what we found is working for the best centres in the market.

I'm happy to visit you at your office or one of your centres. What's the diary like next week for a meeting?"

If I had received that call, I would have responded by saying,

"When can I come and see you?"

But I never did. Because the bankers were too lazy to do the work. They were too lazy to take some time out and think about the challenges I was facing and life from my perspective. They were too lazy to do the work and create a genuinely credible reason for engaging me. They were too lazy to do the work and think about how they could express that in an outbound call that was required to secure a meeting.

Get ready for a little bit of tough love and honesty. If you have a poor lead to meeting conversion, the problem is significantly more likely to be your laziness than the quality of the leads. Here's some good news. In the insurance space, you don't need to do very much work to craft a genuinely credible reason that will increase the likelihood you secure a meeting. You just need to understand how to use ethical influence and how to empathise with what's going through a prospective customer's mind when you call them. Once you've developed ethical and credible reasons, you need to practice your delivery. The way you sound will determine whether the way you propose a meeting or conversation over the phone, and generates a level of certainty that value will be achieved if a prospective customer gives you their valuable time.

I'll show you how to do that, but first let's consider a few common mistakes I want you to avoid. There's a high probability you're making these. If you're not making them, there's a high probability you're not making outbound calls anymore, because you've suffered too much failure in the past. Either way, please take the time out to consider these mistakes and avoid the temptation to jump to the "answers", without reflecting on your current strategies.

COMMON STRATEGIES THAT FAIL THE CREDIBLE REASON TEST

The lazy salesperson in any industry defaults to

"I can save you time and money."

This is the first common mistake I want you to avoid.

I have little doubt that those making cold calls will tell me that they've successfully secured meetings using this reason for calling. They'll defend it on the basis that saving a customer time and money is highly customer centric.

Surely everyone would want to save time and money?

The first challenge I have with this reason for calling is that it's generally not true. Reviewing or considering insurance does and should take up quite a bit of time. And, most effective and customer-centric reviews are going to educate a prospective customer on their real need for cover, which is likely to involve spending more money. That should be enough to knock this one on the head, but there's an even bigger problem this creates for the true insurance professional.

The second reason I strongly recommend against this strategy is that it positions the salesperson and the company they work for as "cheaper". If you work for a company that guarantees to beat any other insurers' pricing with like-for-like cover, please ignore what I've said and tell as many people as you can that you can save them money if they give you a little of their time. But most of you don't work for that insurer. I'm not sure that insurer exists. And if they do, I'm not sure they will survive to pay out on claims made by those that trusted them when purchasing insurance.

When you promote "cheap", you set yourself up to become the victim of cheap purchasing behaviour.

Cheap purchasing behaviour involves demanding more for less, haggling over price, shopping quotes around, delaying decisions and worst of all, focusing more on price than the needs that should drive cover choices. This is not the sort of behaviour you want to promote in your insurance conversations. You and I can't control the providers that have chosen the "cheap" path. We can't control their advertising, and maybe you even work for one of them and need your job. We can't control any of this, but we can choose to be professionals committed to delivering real value in our insurance conversations. That commitment includes engaging people with a more credible and customer-centric reason than "I can save you time and money".

Let me share one exception to this. If you can genuinely and consistently improve people's pricing through more effective structuring, helping them understand what cover they might be paying for that they probably no longer need, or through highlighting insurance you know they are likely to be paying too much for, then it is credible to explain this as a reason for a meeting. If you can help a customer in a specific target market in this way, there's real value in the meeting for them, and these reasons would pass the credibility test.

Salespeople that lack confidence in their ability and feel uncertain about the value of their guidance (or advice) often make the next mistake I want you to avoid. There's a common belief in sales that if you can just get in front of someone for 15 minutes, you'll wow the person so much that they'll want to spend the rest of their day with you. This leads to the next common mistake I want you to avoid.

"If you can just give me 15 minutes of your time I promise you I can show you how to significantly improve your insurance."

This is a common line, spoken with bravado and a story about this amazing sale that happened off the back of a meeting, secured this way.

Once again, I have no doubt there have been sales made leveraging this strategy. But those sales are outlier events, and most of the time, using this strategy is not the difference between securing or failing to secure a meeting. The meetings that are secured this way are significantly more likely to be cancelled and what seemed like a great "play" when you set the meeting often results in wasted time chasing a conversation that was never going to happen. Even if you do secure a meeting using this strategy, what do you think the person's perception will be of your value? If you're willing to do a meeting off the back of them promising only 15 minutes of their time, it's highly likely you're coming across as desperate. There's no need to use this strategy, so take it out of the toolkit and commit to presenting your personal value more effectively.

One last mistake I want you to avoid flows from a high level of confusion around the concept of "adding value". This generally flows from a senior figure in the organisation stating that the sales team needs to "add more value to customers". Sounds great and comes across well in a town hall presentation. The frontline Sales Managers and Team Leaders leave the town hall inspired and committed to adding more value. In the following Monday morning meeting they tell everyone that's what they need to do. An internal coach responsible for scripting, runs with the concept and before you know it, the reason for calling sounds something like,

"We've been adding significant value to other customer's insurance solutions, and I would like to see if we can do the same for you."

Let me give you some insight into the way normal humans outside of your industry process information. When you use a line like this, the prospective customer is saying to themselves,

"What does that mean? I have no idea what adding significant value means?"

Here's the scary and somewhat saddening thing for me. When I ask people using this type of script,

"How are you going to add significant value? Can you give me some specific examples?"

I generally get a blank stare. Or I get,

"Well we might be able to save them some money."

which takes us back to the first mistake I wanted you to avoid. Even scarier, when I ask this question of the Sales Manager telling them to use this script, they generally can't answer the question effectively either! And when I work my way backwards to the person that wrote the script, I get the same blank response. If you give people garbage scripts they will get garbage results.

As a rule, if you can't explain something you're saying to customers, there's a very high probability they don't understand it either. They will nod politely, too embarrassed to ask what you mean, but that doesn't mean they're impressed by your jargon. It generally means they're confused and uncertain and both of those mental states lead to a lack of trust or at the very least, indecision.

These aren't the only mistakes you need to avoid, but let's refocus on what you should be saying and leveraging, as credible reasons for having the insurance conversation. As a professional committed to customer centricity, you won't be surprised that we're going to start with the customer. In particular, the state of mind they're likely to be in when we ask for a meeting or conversation over the phone.

I WASN'T WAITING
FOR YOUR CALL

So much is being written about emotional intelligence and the impact this has on the quality of leadership people experience. This is one of the reasons I'm including commentary aimed at leaders and not just talking to you as a salesperson. The more leaders can empathise with the realities of frontline insurance salespeople, the more effective they'll be at shaping a customer-centric, compliant and high-performance sales culture.

As a salesperson, the more you can empathise with the people you want to engage in insurance conversations, the more successful you'll be at securing their valuable time. When you call a prospective customer (including someone that has been referred to you), you need to understand and empathise with two things.

The first is their situation and the second is how they will naturally respond to your call. The more we understand how these two factors will influence a customer's response, the more effectively we can plan for and execute an effective engagement strategy.

In relation to a person's situation, a mobile world means when we connect with someone on the phone they could be anywhere and be doing anything. We want to avoid their first impression of us as being pushy or desperate to speak. I suggest your approach should include using a strategy to confirm a person can speak, before jumping into the reason for calling. I've had numerous debates over the years that go something like this.

> **ME** "Professionals aren't desperate or pushy. This means before we launch into the call, we should confirm that the customer is able to speak. That means asking "Do you have a moment?", before we launch into our reason for calling."

> **SALESPEOPLE** *"But Dean, if we give them an "out", they will always say they're too busy, and it's better to get straight into your spiel and not give them a chance to say no to the call."*

I would argue strongly, that it's rare that a surprise attack on the phone yields a truly customer-centric result for the prospective customer. People may politely listen to you, but in their heart, they probably feel like you cheated to capture their attention. I can appreciate the fear of confirming a person has time to speak, but my position on this is that customer centricity should triumph. The very common, pushy approach in many insurance call centres, should be replaced with a more professional and customer-centric approach.

The second thing we need to empathise with is the customer's mental state when we call them. Unfortunately, it is very unlikely that just before you called them they were thinking,

"I hope someone gives me a call about my insurance today."

It's also very likely that they've had bad experiences in the past. It's likely that the insurance conversation is something they've been subconsciously avoiding.

These factors mean a defensive or dismissive response is likely. And that's a big point. When you start to see, hear and emotionally experience defensive and dismissive behaviour, as a natural human reaction, it removes a lot of the emotion from common objections to the conversation. None of these factors makes engagement easier and all point to the need to "do the work" if you want to improve call to insurance conversation/ meeting ratios.

REDUCING DEFENSIVE RESPONSES AND BEHAVIOURS

When you call a prospective customer out of the blue, there are three things that they need to rapidly understand if you want to avoid a naturally defensive response.

1. Who you are and where you're calling from.

2. How you're connected.

3. If you're going to waste their time.

People naturally suffer from what I call "stranger danger". The faster you can help them answer these three questions, the more likely it is they will take down their defences. To make it easier for a customer to rapidly answer these three questions you need to be strategic about the first 5 – 10 seconds of the call.

First, you need to be good at explaining who you are and where you're from. When I've reviewed calls, it never ceases to amaze me how many people fail in this area. I literally can't understand their name or the name of the company they're calling from. In general, the fewer words, the better – and shortening titles and division names is often a step in the right direction. As an exercise, listen to several recorded calls (if you have access) and notice both the difference between introductions and how the better people are doing it differently.

Second, and more important, is creating a connection. The faster and more effectively you make a connection to the customer, the faster they put aside their defences. When we do scripting workshops, this is generally not a strategy that's being used, and where it is, it's rarely used effectively. Let me give you an example relating to a referred lead. Imagine John Jones had suggested you call his sister Mary Jones.

A disconnected entry would be something like this.

SALESPERSON *"Hi, is that Mary Jones I'm speaking to?"*

MARY "Yes, it is." (Wary and uncomfortable tone)

SALESPERSON *"Hi Mary, how's your day?"*

MARY "Good thanks." (Thinking – who is this?)

SALESPERSON *"That's great Mary. My name is Dan Disconnected, and I'm from the Life Division of We Want to Sell You Insurance. The reason I'm calling today is…"*

Now let's contrast this with a more connected engagement strategy.

SALESPERSON *"Hi Mary, this is Christine Connected, your brother John suggested I give you a call. Do you have a moment?"*

MARY "OK. What's it about?"

SALESPERSON *"Thanks Mary, I've been helping your brother John with a review of his insurance. He was surprised by the gap between the cover he thought he had and what was in his current policies. He suggested I might be able to do the same for you. How long has it been since you reviewed your life policies in detail?"*

Let me make an important point here from a compliance and ethics point of view. Don't lie about what you're doing, or not doing, for customers. But, if you are getting great feedback from customers and they're surprised by the gaps in cover you've helped them understand, then use this as a credible reason to be engaging others in a similar situation. In this situation where we are using the brother's name, we would obviously need to make sure we had their permission to do so.

On a point of compliance, I've seen some pretty strong policies put in place that stop insurance salespeople from asking for or using referrals as a reason for calling someone. So, as with all the strategies I share in this book, please check in with the compliance team on your company's policy.

I imagine those of you that don't get many referrals, might be thinking,

"That's great Dean, but I don't get any referrals."

The first thing I would say to you is,

"Why not?"

But let's not get off track. Here's an example of how you could create a connection if you were getting leads from another part of your business.

SALESPERSON *"Hi Mary, it's Jenny from Acme Bank. Bill Jones takes care of your business banking, and he suggested I give you a call. Do you have a moment?*

MARY "OK. What's it about?"

SALESPERSON *"Thanks Mary, I've been helping several of Bill's other business customers to do free reviews on their personal insurance and mapping that to what's going on in their business. Several of his business customers that have done the review, told me they've been too busy with their business to really think about their personal policies. Have you had time to do a detailed review recently?"*

Once again, don't lie (this includes making things up) about what you're doing and achieving for customers. If you personally don't have a recent customer that was too busy to do a review on their personal policies, don't be defeated by this. There's still a credible, ethical and compliant way forward with this connection strategy. If you speak to several of your colleagues and one of them tells you all about a new customer that was too busy running their business to do a review on their personal insurance, you can change the script to something like this.

SALESPERSON *"Thanks Mary, the part of the bank I work for has been helping our business customers to do free reviews on their personal insurance and mapping that to what's going on in their business. Something that business customers are telling us is they've been too busy with their business to really* *think about their personal policies. Have you had time to do a detailed review recently?"*

Rather than speaking about your personal experiences, you can legitimately take ownership of the experiences and results of your colleagues.

Some of you are possibly feeling jealous that you don't work for a bank that gives you referrals and might be thinking,

"That's great Dean, but I don't work for a bank"

or

"That's great Dean but I hardly ever get leads from the bankers I work with."

Once again, the first thing I would say to you is,

"Why not?"

But let's not get off track. Here's an example of how you could create a connection if you don't get any leads. Let's say you just put insurance in place for a baker. You could put together a list of other bakers and target leads in the food industry. Your connection strategy would sound something like this.

SALESPERSON *"Hi Betty, it's Jenny from Acme Bank. I've been working with another baker down the road from your store, and I thought it made sense to give you a call. Do you have a moment?"*

MARY *"OK. What's it about?"*

SALESPERSON *"Thanks, Betty. As I mentioned, I've just completed a personal insurance review for another baker in your area, and they were very surprised to see the results of the review and several risks they hadn't* *covered. Have you had time to do a detailed review recently?"*

Another common disconnect is when people hear an accent, different to the local accent they're accustomed to. In the multicultural Australian environment, many insurance salespeople working in call centres experience a disconnect because people assume they're calling from a foreign call centre. The following is a great strategy for overcoming this early in the call.

SALESPERSON *"Hi Betty, it's Jenny from the Adelaide team at Acme bank. I've been working over the phone, with another baker down the road from your store. I thought it made sense to give you a call. Do you have a moment?"*

MARY "Ok. What's it about?"

SALESPERSON *"Thanks, Betty. As I mentioned, I've just completed a personal insurance review for another baker in your area. They were very surprised to see the results of the review and several risks they hadn't covered. Have you had time to do a detailed review recently?"*

The big point here is that you need to make sure you create a connection to help the customer answer,

"How am I connected to you?"

very early in the call. The more effectively you do this, the more likely it is they will remove their defences and engage with you in the insurance conversation or a conversation about the value of a meeting.

The third question a customer is trying to rapidly consider and answer is,

"Are you going to waste my time?"

People don't fear cold calls and other forms of approach by insurance salespeople. What they fear is people wasting their time, and worse, taking advantage of them.

The way you deliver the entry to the call, the confidence and comfort you project, and the clarity of your speech, will all dramatically impact the way the customer subconsciously answers this question. To deliver confidently, you need to practise! And importantly, you need to practise out loud. If making these sorts of calls is part of the way you sell insurance you should be practising at least once a week for a minimum of 30 minutes. This should include calling a recorded line and listening back to your calls. It should include peer review and honest feedback. And the focus should be on achieving excellence rather than not being bad at it. I'll talk more about the importance of deliberately creating a perception of credibility in the next chapter.

WHAT MAKES A REASON CREDIBLE?

As I've gone to pains to point out, the more customer centric the reason for the call, the more credibility it will have in the mind of the person you're calling. Having said that, credibility is a perception, so there are several ethical persuasion strategies you can and should be leveraging in the creation of your credible reasons. These should not be considered (or used) as tricks to get people to talk to you. At the core of your reason for calling there needs to be something of genuine value to the customer. My personal belief is that it's the rare person you speak to that has genuinely made a fully educated set of decisions on the cover they've put in place. This means there is nearly always a valuable reason to engage with an insurance professional in the insurance conversation.

Strategies that you should consider leveraging to make your credible reasons more ethically persuasive include the following.

Connection

As you've seen from the examples I've shared, clearly stating the connection between you and the person you call makes it more likely they will respond positively to your call and engage with you. A connection can be created through the referrer's name. It can be created through another relationship they have within your business and the mention of this. It can even be created through a product they haven't purchased from your business.

SALESPERSON *"Hi Bill. We're touching base with all our customers that have their mortgages with us but haven't taken any personal insurance protection under an Acme Bank policy. Do you have a quick moment to discuss that?"*

BILL "Sure. What's it about?"

SALESPERSON *"Thanks Bill, two reasons for the call. The first is just to say thanks for choosing us as your mortgage provider. We know it's competitive out there and really appreciate you choosing us. (Pause – you'll be amazed at how customers respond/engage in conversation accordingly) The second reason we're calling is to make sure you've reviewed your personal insurances, having regard to the new home and the mortgage you've put in place. Have you done a detailed review of your personal insurances since you moved into the house?"*

Reciprocity

When you turn up to a relationship with something to give, it sends a very strong signal to the prospective customer that they are likely to achieve value out of a relationship with you. When you turn up to a relationship hoping to "take", people generally pick up on this subconsciously and become highly defensive and dismissive.

At a base level, please take this phrase out of your calls.

SALESPERSON *"Hi Bill. Can I just take five minutes of your time to ask you about..."?*

The word "take" is something you need to avoid in most selling situations. More importantly, creating the perception that you have something to give, often triggers a positive response in people you call. This is even more likely where what you are offering is positioned as having value. If we go back to an earlier script I shared, notice the implied reciprocity (something of value to give) in this script.

SALESPERSON *"Thanks Mary, the part of the bank I work for has been helping our business customers to do free reviews on their personal insurance and mapping that to what's going on in their business. Something that business customers are telling us is they've been too busy with their business to really think about their personal policies. Have you had time to do a detailed review recently?"*

Social Proof

People feel more comfortable when their behaviour matches the behaviour of other people like them. You've probably had people asking,

"Well, what amount of insurance are other people like me taking out?"

This is a natural request because there's a perceived safety in doing what the herd is doing. It's also why selling insurance is so challenging. Most people are ignoring it and assuming there's plenty of cover in their superannuation or group cover policies. And when most people are assuming this, it feels safe to make the same assumption.

As I mentioned earlier, don't make up social proof and say,

"Everybody is…"

if this is not factual. That's not ethical and it's not compliant. But where you can ethically and compliantly leverage social proof, make sure you mention that you're solving problems for people just like the person you're speaking to. You'll notice there is an element of social proof in the script I've shared above. Generally, when you can synthesise two to three ethical persuasion strategies into a scripted strategy you significantly increase the likelihood of success.

Authority

People tend to respond positively to the requests of people they perceive to be experts and those they perceive to have authority. Strategically, this means where you can ethically create a sense of authority or expertise, you should. At a base level, the language you use, the way you speak and the pace at which you speak should create the perception that you're confident in engaging the person you're calling. Removing "ums" and "ahs" is a good place to begin.

Generally, the use of fewer words creates a greater sense of authority, as do pauses and asking questions with an expectation that they will be answered.

If you have a title that suggests you have authority, you should use it. An example would be something like this.

SALESPERSON *"Thanks Bill. Mark, your Relationship Manager, may have mentioned I would give you a call. My role as an Insurance Specialist within Acme is to make sure all our customers are fully educated on some of the risks they should consider and their options. Another thing I'm responsible for is making sure you have a clear understanding of how much and what type of insurance you're eligible for. Have you had any feedback on what insurance you're eligible for?"*

Scarcity

People will want something a lot more if they believe it is difficult to get. Where time to secure an opportunity is perceived to be running out, people are also more likely to consider and take actions. This is a strategy that must be used ethically. If there's any doubt in your mind, don't use it! Having said that, where there is genuine scarcity, you should ethically use it as it promotes a greater willingness to participate in a thorough review of needs and cover options.

An example of how you might ethically use this is as follows:

SALESPERSON *"Thanks Jenny, the reason I'm calling is I do a lot of work with people aged 30 – 35 that have recently purchased a home. A lot of insurance professionals don't focus on this market, because to be honest, the policy premiums tend to be smaller and that means they earn less. The reason I like helping people like you is there's an opportunity to get insurance in place at a lower cost than when you're 40, and ideally before there are any health issues that could prevent you from getting access to the insurance you want. I'm not sure what you're eligible for, but if you're happy to answer a few questions for me I can let you know right now. Can I start with..."*

This isn't a comprehensive list of all the strategies you can use to build a credible reason, but that should be more than enough for most of you to significantly improve your ability to engage someone in the insurance conversation. Ethically leveraging persuasion strategies, developing scripts, aligning quality assurance processes and improving the coaching of these scripts is at the core of our work within our insurance customers. And the return on getting this part of the sales process right, for both salespeople and the organisation, is significant to say the least.

The customer-centric way starts with engaging – using customer-focused credible reasons.

WRAP UP

I've scratched the surface of a very big topic in this chapter, but I'm confident this should give you a deep enough understanding of the concept and how to apply it. My philosophy is that salespeople generally aren't lazy, they're just not motivated.

The more work you do on building credible reasons to connect with your target market, the more confident and motivated you become to make that call. The more you practise this, the more you'll progress towards excellence in delivering your credible reason over the phone and in person. Excellence in any skill grows with both confidence and motivation.

You can be compliant in this area and achieve excellence in your lead/call to insurance conversation or meeting conversion ratio. Do the work and build your skills in this area. If this is the only thing you improve, it is a skill that will reward you for the rest of your sales career.

CHAPTER NINE

BUILDING RAPPORT AND CREDIBILITY

HOW TRUSTWORTHY ARE YOU?

I have no doubt your immediate reaction to this was,

"I'm totally trustworthy, Dean."

But here's the challenge in sales. It's not about how trustworthy you think or even know you are – it's about how trustworthy the people you engage in the insurance conversation think and feel you are. When selling to a person, their perception of your trustworthiness is what defines the level of trust in the relationship. And often, success or failure is about a judgement they make about your trustworthiness in the first five to ten seconds of engaging with you. Sometimes people that don't really trust you, can't even explain why they don't trust you.

This is not fair. Don't expect it to be. The more frustrated you are about this, the less resilient you are and the less constructive and intelligent you'll be about addressing this challenge.

Instead, I need you to make a commitment. I need you to commit to becoming a student of trust. I need you to chase every bit of knowledge and research you can on the subject. I need you to start paying attention to what others do to build your trust, and anything that diminishes or destroys your trust for other people. I need you to do the same in relation to your trust for companies and brands. And, I need you to commit to developing your awareness and skills, in relation to deliberately building trust, in any situation you find yourself in.

Building trust needs to be a habit rather than a set of strategies you roll out when you're trying to sell something. Being perceived as trustworthy requires you to make trust-building habits a part of who you are. Are you willing to make that commitment?

Do you truly deserve the trust of those you engage in the insurance conversation?

Trust, rapport and credibility is a huge subject. There are many great books in this area and I want to avoid trying to write one in this chapter. What I want you to take away from this chapter is a thirst for more knowledge, the ability to ethically employ strategies that build trust and a commitment to making these a part of who you are as a person, inside and outside of your work.

CAN YOU REALLY "BUILD" TRUST?

The simple answer is "Yes – you can".

Additionally, there are habits and behaviours you can adopt, that will impact how rapidly you build trust with another person.

Whether that's face to face or over the phone. There are habits and behaviours you can avoid, that will reduce the likelihood that you will diminish or damage trust levels. And for all of us, including me, there are always behaviours we can change to improve our results in this area.

There are two drivers of trust levels when two people interact. Both are critically important and both must be in place for trust to be achieved in a relationship.

The two drivers are the level of rapport and the perceived level of credibility. Interestingly this goes both ways. If you're not in rapport with a customer or you don't perceive they are credible, it's highly doubtful there will be trust in the relationship.

Many salespeople mistake high levels of rapport for high levels of trust. But without perceived credibility there will not be a high level of trust. Let me explain. Most of you will have several great friends. And I'm betting one of those friends is someone you love spending time with. I bet you would have them over to your house anytime. If you have kids, you may even be happy to let them babysit for you. But let me ask you a serious question.

Would you go into partnership in a business with this friend?

For many of you, the answer will be "no way".

Generally, this is linked to a lack of perceived credibility in some aspect of their behaviour, intelligence or character. This doesn't necessarily mean you think they're a bad person. It just means at some level you're not prepared to trust them with your financial future.

My point is that you can be in a massive state of rapport with someone, but not commercially trust them enough to go into business with them. It's the same with prospective customers.

Just because someone really likes talking to you, has a laugh with you and engages with you socially, doesn't mean they trust you enough to take care of their insurance. It doesn't mean they trust you enough to share their financial information. It doesn't mean they trust you enough to share their fears and hopes for their family, should something happen to them. It doesn't mean they're open to discussing their death with you.

Don't mistake rapport for trust. Trust requires both a high level of rapport and a high level of perceived credibility.

DO PEOPLE NEED TO TRUST YOU TO BUY FROM YOU?

The sad answer is, no. People can and do buy from those they don't completely trust.

In an interesting piece of research[9] that was shared at a conference I spoke at many years ago, managers from over 3000 companies were surveyed around the level of trust they had for salespeople they had purchased from in the previous two years. The survey was focused on the highest level of trust they had for any salesperson they had purchased from in the previous two years. Given the focus was on the highest level of trust, my expectation was that at least one person that sold them something would have achieved "complete trust", which was one of the answers available.

What astonished me was that only 3 percent of managers reported that any salesperson had achieved this level of trust with them. Sixty-eight percent of the managers reported that the highest level of trust achieved by any of the salespeople they had purchased from was "rarely or not at all". People are very unlikely to trust those they know are trying to sell them something. Please don't think this gets you off the hook from having to "do the work" in committing to improve your trust-building skills and habits. For me, it highlights just how important and differentiating the ability to rapidly build trust can be.

People are far more likely to trust you if they feel you're helping them to buy the right cover, rather than selling them insurance.

HOW DO I BUILD RAPPORT?

A better question to consider is,

"How are you currently building rapport?"

Take a little time out to consider this. Take yourself back to the last meeting or call you had with a customer or a prospective customer and write down as many points as you can on things you did that you know built rapport. Be as honest as possible in doing this reflective exercise. When I ask people to do this immediately after engaging another person, most are challenged to come up with more than five things they did deliberately to build higher levels of rapport. If you're committed to a standard of excellence, this doesn't cut it.

Think about the last meeting you had (phone or face to face), and answer honestly whether you deliberately engaged in these types of behaviours.

1. Did you take the time to make sure they knew your name? (Did they use it?)

2. Did you use their name during the conversation?

3. Did you "shake hands" effectively? (How much connection did you experience before you started explaining the reason for the call or meeting?)

4. Who did most of the talking? Did you let them talk at all?

5. Did you paraphrase what they were saying, or say something to let them know you had heard what they said?

6. Did you deliberately and credibly agree with something they said?

7. What language did you use to confirm you were listening and agreeing? Did you grunt or did you say something like 'absolutely' or 'spot on' or 'good one'?

8. Were you using visual cues like nodding and smiling and making eye contact to show you were engaged and enjoying speaking to them? (Answer this even if it was a phone call.)

9. Were you deliberately using the same language as theirs?

10. Did you adapt your tone to match theirs?

11. Did you speed up or slow down your pace of speech to match or mirror theirs?

12. Did you adapt your volume to match theirs?

13. Did you adapt your posture to mirror or match their body language? (Answer this even if it was a phone call.)

14. Did you mirror or match their energy level?

15. Was your posture open and facing them or was it closed and pointed away from them? (Even if you were on the phone – did your posture suggest you were open and interested?)

And if you think the list is a little long, we're just getting started. There are over 75 years of research on what builds higher levels of rapport and what's referred to by psychologists as "liking". Like I said, I'm doing my best to avoid writing a book inside this chapter, but I do want to make sure you understand the four key drivers of rapport/liking and how to apply it.

The research tells us that higher levels of rapport/liking generate the following behaviours in the other person we're engaging in the insurance conversation.

1. They become more supportive of anything you propose

2. They are more likely to agree with what you say

3. They are more likely to share information with you

4. They are more likely to let you know if they have any challenges or concerns

5. They are less likely to do anything that would harm you (including shopping around)

Imagine if you could honestly describe every customer and prospective customer relationship that way. Imagine how much more fun your role would be. Imagine how much easier it would be to help people buy the right cover. Imagine how rewarding it would be from both a relationship perspective and a financial perspective. The customer-centric professional expects this to be the nature of their relationships with customers and prospective customers. And that expectation comes with high standards in relation to their personal rapport-building behaviours and habits.

FOUR KEY
DRIVERS OF RAPPORT
AND LIKING

I want to make the point one more time. See these as behaviours you're committed to making into habits. Think about them as habits you're committed to making a part of the person you are. If you can achieve this, success in your entire life will flow from relationships that cause others to want to help you and want to be helped by you. For the sake of simplicity, if I speak about rapport

I'm also speaking about creating a state of liking between you and the person you're engaging in the insurance conversation.

Key Driver #1
Similarity

The first key driver of rapport is the perception that there is a high level of similarity between yourself and the other person.

You've probably experienced moments when the energy in your conversations completely changed, just after you established common ground. That could be something as simple as both having children, growing up in a similar area, holidaying in a similar location or any other experience that you have in common. I shouldn't have to say this but… PLEASE don't make things up, to be similar to (liked by) the person to whom you're speaking. Life is much easier when you don't tell lies, because you don't have to remember what lies you told to the hundreds of people you should be speaking to! And you're obviously behaving in a compliant and trustworthy manner.

Similarity in experiences, and common ground, are triggers for rapport, but an even stronger trigger is the perception that you have similar goals and similar values. When people believe that your beliefs and view of the world match theirs, this subconsciously triggers higher levels of rapport and liking. When they perceive you're genuinely trying to help them achieve what matters to them, they're more likely to engage fully.

Importantly, this also means that the more you can minimise the differences between you and the other person, the better the state of rapport with you. This means you need to avoid disagreeing with them and making them wrong. As we like to say at SalesROI, you can never "win" an argument with a customer. You need to be aware of the language you use and the way you speak. Ideally, do your best to credibly match the other person. You need to be aware of differences in communication preferences and develop your ability to credibly adapt your style to reduce difference and maximise similarities.

There is so much value in committing to a deeper understanding of this driver of rapport. Importantly, there is so much value in becoming more personally aware of your own communication habits and how these might create a perception of difference when engaging prospective and existing customers. I know this because I have made so many mistakes in this area over the 30 plus years of my career.

Key Driver #2
Exchange

Exchange relates to the two-way interaction between two or more humans. Research has confirmed that the more often two people engage in exchange, the more likely it is that they will be in a state of rapport.

If you buy coffee from the same place every day, you probably feel like you're in a state of rapport with the person that serves you, despite not really knowing them that well. The simple lesson from this is that the more often we engage with the prospective customer to help them through their insurance purchasing journey, the more likely it is they will feel like they have a stronger sense of rapport with us.

But quality and what's often referred to as the "richness" of the exchange also has a significant impact on the level of rapport achieved through the exchange. Going back to our coffee example, smart café owners improve the quality of exchange by remembering your name and using it to say hello. They remember how you like your coffee and proactively ask,

"The usual?"

The good ones even know what time you come down every day and have it ready to go!

What are your exchange habits? When you buy something at the supermarket do you look the person serving you in the eye? Do you say a sincere hello? If you ask them how their day is going do you really listen to their response? Do you go out of your way to thank them and do your best to improve their day? Or do you ignore them, talk on your phone and maybe go through the motions of pretend exchange because it's the polite thing to do? Remember, excellence requires you to make this a habit and places such as the supermarket are fantastic places to practise.

A subset of richness worth considering is proximity. The closer two people are to one another the more likely it is that exchange will generate rapport. Sending emails to one another does not bring you very "close" to the customer. Speaking to them on the phone brings you closer. Speaking on online video brings you even closer. Getting face time with them brings you closer still. And when you meet them face to face in their office or home you're really close. Consider the way you're currently exchanging with prospective and existing customers. Are there ways you could be "closer" to the customer, when you're engaging them in the insurance conversation?

Key Driver #3
Praise

Do your customers know what it is you like about them?

When you tell someone you like something about them (praise), it triggers off a reciprocal response that causes them to look for something they like about you. This increases the level of rapport.

The funny thing about this is that I've seen research that suggests even if they know you're "sucking up" to them it still builds rapport.

But, it damages your credibility, and as we now know, that damages overall trust.

Consider this, when was the last time you praised someone sincerely? Please – stop and be honest about this.

As with all the other strategies we're discussing, it is the commitment to turning these into habits that will enable you to translate these behaviours into rapid and deep trust with every person you engage. Becoming more aware of what could and should be praised will change your life. The person that effortlessly sees the good in others effortlessly generates the praise of others. My belief is that if someone is willing to put the effort into protecting those they love, that is worthy of praise. You may be the only person that really knows what they've committed to and you're in a unique position to sincerely praise them for putting the needs of others ahead of their own.

Key Driver #4
Admiration

What do the people you sell to admire about you?

When I ask this question at conferences, I often get quite a few weird looks from the crowd. Especially in Australia, where we suffer from the tall poppy syndrome and get very concerned about others knowing that they are very good at something. Research is telling us that the more someone admires you, the more they want to be in a state of rapport with you. We like to associate with people we admire. We like to spend time with people we admire. We go out of our way to do business with people we admire. And we put more effort into introducing people we admire.

Maybe people admire your commitment to your profession. Maybe they admire the way you educate them through great questions rather than telling them things. Maybe they admire the way you effortlessly communicate and present solutions in easy to understand ways. Maybe they admire the effort you put into making sure they considered everything relevant to determining how much cover was required rather than rushing to sell them something. Maybe they admire how energetic you are or how much you remember about them from the previous conversation. The point I'm trying to make here is that you don't need to be a national sporting champion or a rock star to be admired.

What could you do at your next meeting that would cause someone to admire you and the way you help people buy the right cover?

RAPPORT BUILDING SOUNDS LIKE HARD WORK

If all this sounds like it takes effort, that's because it does. But the returns you'll get in every aspect of your life are enormous if you can make rapport-building behaviours part of your habits.

If you're in sales (as I am), there's a high probability that you think you're much better at rapport building than you really are. There's a high probability you think people like you, much more than they really do. It protects our self-esteem and enables us to keep engaging more prospective customers. But you need to avoid making the common mistake of thinking you know all you need to know, and do all you need to do in relation to building rapport and creating the liking dynamic between you and the people you engage. Do the work. Commit to being a better person, and others are more likely to commit to you being a partner in their insurance purchasing journey.

DO PEOPLE
THINK OF YOU AS
AN "EXPERT"?

One of the things I like to remind everyone who sells, is that people who are perceived to be experts tend to get paid more than those perceived to be friends.

My point is that your rapport-building skills will add significant value to your relationships, but it is your credibility-building skills that will have the greatest financial impact. People are also more likely to be guided by (and where advice can be offered, more likely to take the advice of) those they perceive to be experts. So, creating the perception that you're an expert in the insurance space, will have a significant impact on your ability to help people make the right choices and buy the right solutions.

I think one of the most exciting things about the insurance industry is that you don't need a lot of qualifications to be able to sell insurance solutions and help people buy the right cover. I think one of the most challenging aspects of being in the insurance industry is that the lack of required qualifications means that people don't think of insurance salespeople as experts. I'm sure several financial planners and advisors with qualifications are challenged by what I've just said. But let's face it, financial planners and advisors in the financial services space are consistently rating in the bottom 20 percent of surveys that rate trust levels by industry. Whether you have lots of qualifications or not, the default perception of people buying insurance is that you're not an expert. You must accept this. Once you've accepted it, you'll be prepared to do the work that's required to create the perception of expertise.

Now let's consider what that work involves.

WHAT DRIVES CREDIBILITY AND THE PERCEPTION OF EXPERTISE?

Nothing will impact the perception of your expertise more than your ability to ask and answer questions.

I want you to lock that into your brain and commit to working on this area of your skills. Your ability to ask high-quality, customer-centric, educational and insightful questions will dramatically impact the quality of the insurance conversation and customer experience. Your ability to listen to customers, answer the questions they've asked and create certainty will have a similar impact. I can train you on how to do that effectively. The thing I can't train you on, however, is genuinely caring about the customer's situation and asking and answering questions in a manner that displays appropriate levels of care and curiosity.

I am constantly frustrated by compliance-driven scripts, lazy questioning strategies and budget-focused sales paths that are not only condoned by organisations but are also actively coached. These destroy the credibility of the insurance salesperson using them and, while sales may be made, customer experience and the quality of insurance solutions suffer. The following list of strategies and thoughts is not just for you as an insurance salesperson. It's also for you as a person.

A huge part of success in sales should be the ability to sleep peacefully at night, knowing that you've delivered the right solution to those whom you've helped buy the right insurance. Some of the most rewarding experiences you will have in your career will involve the death of a person you have insured – but only if you helped them buy the right cover.

Don't think of this as a list of strategies. Think of it as a personal code that protects your integrity and ability to work in the industry.

You need to see both as your most valuable assets; and when you truly do, results will follow.

This list is also for the sales managers, coaches and senior leaders who need to take complete responsibility for the way their people sell. If you're committed to a truly customer-centric approach, you need to become honest about whether your focus on compliance is blinding you to practices and behaviours that are legal but not truly ethical or credible.

Experts Understand Customer Needs

I think Covey[10] said it best, when he shared the concept of,

"Seek to understand before seeking to be understood"

in his groundbreaking book, *The Seven Habits of Highly Successful People.* If you haven't read this book yet, make sure it's the next on your list. This is a timeless manual on how to be a better person, live a better life and enjoy greater success.

The more a customer thinks you really understand them on both a rational level *("If I die, my partner will need to be able to pay out the mortgage on the family home")* and an emotional level *("That's important to me because we have three children"),* the more credibility you'll have in the relationship. People who do the work to genuinely understand the customer are significantly more likely to enjoy expert status in the mind of the prospective customer. This remains important throughout the ongoing years of the relationship. People's lives change, and the insurance salesperson who diligently checks in and genuinely takes the time out to re-engage and understand what's happened in the past year and may happen in the coming year retains expert status.

Those who fail to call often get relegated to "someone who sold me something" status.

The bottom line on this is that if you have not created a dynamic with the customer that includes them perceiving that you understand their needs, they're very unlikely to think of you as an expert with any value to offer. You cannot be customer centric or credible if you don't understand the customer and what's driving their needs.

Experts Don't
Provide "Quotes"

When a customer rings you and says,

"Can I get a quote for $500,000 of life insurance?"

the worst thing you can do for your credibility is to say,

"Yes".

Let me explain: nobody respects, values or thinks highly of those who simply provide pricing when asked for a "quote". If people see you as a quoting machine, they will treat you as a quoting machine. If you walked into your doctor and said,

"Can you give me a prescription for 20 tablets of penicillin?"

and they simply said,

"Yes"

what would you think of their intellect? If you walked into your lawyer and simply said,

"Please sue Billy Bloggs for $20,000"

and they said,

"Yes"

did up the documents and gave you a bill for $3,000, how would you feel about paying that bill?

Whether you're licensed to provide advice or not, you need to move as far away from the "quoting machine" perception as possible. If you sell insurance over the phone, let me explain how you do this. If you don't sell insurance over the phone, read on anyway.

First, here's a very direct strategy for letting someone know there's more to providing the right cover than simply providing a price:

PROSPECTIVE CUSTOMER
"Can I get a quote for $500,000 of insurance?"

SALESPERSON *"I can certainly help you with that. Is it just about the price of the insurance, or do you need to be sure you'll be able to make a claim on it if something happens?" (Pause – stay quiet!)*

PROSPECTIVE CUSTOMER
"What do you mean?"

SALESPERSON *"I can give you a price on what we call guaranteed cover, but it will exclude a significant number of claims, including anything related to a previous medical condition. If you buy on price, you need to be aware that making a claim could be very difficult for the people you're trying to protect. But if we can go through a process to determine what we can cover, I can give you a lot more certainty on what the insurance does and doesn't cover. Is it OK if I ask you a few questions?"*

For some of you, that might seem a little aggressive. My opinion is that anyone that opens up with,

"Just give me a price"

is the aggressive one. And, more importantly, this is a very strong signal that they're ignorant about their real needs. It's also a signal that one of your competitors may be selling to them in a manner that is a lot more focused on price than on their needs. If you provide them with this explanation and they still just want a price, I'm not sure you want them as a customer.

I can appreciate that some of you won't want to be this confrontational. So, here's a softer strategy for taking control of the discussion and letting people know you're a professional who wants to help them buy the right cover.

PROSPECTIVE CUSTOMER
"Can I get a quote for $500,000 of insurance?"

SALESPERSON *"Sure, I can do that for you. Can I ask who I'm speaking to?"*

PROSPECTIVE CUSTOMER
"Betty Johnson."

SALESPERSON *"Thanks, Betty. How did you come to amount of $500,000?"*

PROSPECTIVE CUSTOMER
"I just need a quote, thanks."

SALESPERSON *"I can definitely give you information on what the premiums will be. I'll just need to understand a little more about your personal situation – stuff like age and current health. Is that OK?"*

PROSPECTIVE CUSTOMER
"OK."

SALESPERSON *(Ask your fundamental health questions.)*

SALESPERSON *"Great, Betty. I've entered all of that in and premiums should be up soon. It sounds like you've already got a price from someone else. Is that right?"*

PROSPECTIVE CUSTOMER
"Yes, but I'm not sharing that with you."

SALESPERSON *"Understand completely, Betty. I just want to make sure of two things: first, that we're comparing apples with apples and I'm giving you a price on the same type of cover. The other thing I want to make sure of is that you understand what's not covered. I would hate for you or your family to make a claim and find out you're not covered because that wasn't explained to you effectively. Is there something particular like a mortgage you want to be paid out with the insurance?"*

Don't get sucked into quoting early in the relationship. Once you've fallen into this trap, it is very unlikely that you'll get the opportunity to display the value of your expertise and needs-analysis skills.

Experts Don't Assume that People Want to Save Money

I may be a little guilty of behaviour associated with being a "control freak", but I'm not alone. When any of my advisors make a decision on my behalf without consulting me, I get very upset. Like all humans, I have a need for options and a desire to feel like I'm the one making choices. I'll admit this is rarely the case when my better half, Tereza, is involved! But in business, if you take that away from me, you're not providing me with a customer-centric experience. You may not breach your compliance requirements, but I also believe this is not very ethical either.

An example of this occurred with the insurance salesperson who previously took care of our business-related life insurance. He was sacked for several reasons, but the one that sits in my mind, related to an emailed renewal notice on our life policies. These policies covered the buy/sell agreement on the partnership shares in our business.

His first mistake, on quite a significant policy, was that he couldn't be bothered to make an effort to call us to discuss our renewal. If he had, we probably would have increased the amount covered, to reflect the growth in the business and the increased value of the shares. (Which we've done subsequently with another insurance salesperson).

The second mistake, which really upset me, was that the amount covered in the renewal notice we were asked to authorise, was for less than the amount we initially insured. I'm often not great with the detail, but I picked this up and asked my business partner, who had the relationship with the previous insurance salesperson, to check out what was going on. It turned out that the insurance salesperson had unilaterally decided we would prefer to be paying the same premium costs, and had reduced the amount of cover to achieve this. This was completely inconsistent with the reason we had put the insurance in place. It was completely inconsistent with the growing nature of our business. It was completely inconsistent with the way we buy on value rather than price. And, it was completely inconsistent with the way we had treated him during the purchase process a year earlier.

I had no relationship with this advisor, but I can tell you that his credibility was destroyed because of this assumption.

Experts
Give Options

What should he have done? The credible advisor would have called us to discuss it rather than sending a notice hoping we would just approve it so he could get his ongoing commissions. The call would have been focused on finding out about what had happened in the business over the year, whether we or our financial advisors perceived that the shares had increased in value and what our thoughts were about the adequacy of the cover. But let's put that to the side and just consider how he could have handled his complete failure more effectively:

> **US** "There's definitely strong growth, but we're both comfortable leaving the current policies in place."

> **SALESPERSON** *"Understand completely, Dean. Can I just ask, is that about maintaining the current premiums and not having to pay extra or is it that you feel a hundred percent comfortable with the payout on the policies in relation to the current value of the shares?"*

> **US** "It's a bit of both."

> **SALESPERSON** *"OK. There are two options on how to take care of the insurance this year. If we keep the current payouts in place, there's a small increase in the cost of premiums to reflect that you're both a year older. I can let you know exactly what that increase will be over the next few days. There is a second option that you should know about. If you want to keep the premium payments the same and preserve cash flow, you could slightly drop the amount of cover to retain the same premium cost as last year. Which would you prefer?"*

If you're an advisor that can provide advice, don't make the mistake of thinking that includes making decisions for the people you're charged with protecting and providing for. This is not part of the relationship and is not customer centric, no matter how well-intentioned you were.

Often there's belief that people will not buy from you if you sell to needs rather than starting with what someone can afford. Recently, I've also noticed that regulations around the requirement to confirm affordability are creating budget-focused sales behaviours that avoid needs-based conversations. Unfortunately, this non-customer-centric behaviour is being supported by compliance and those responsible for quality assurance. If you face these challenges, I hope you're wondering how to comply, focus on needs and be successful in making sales. Let me give you an example of how to remain customer centric and achieve both compliance and the sale.

SALESPERSON *"Mary, I'm not licensed to recommend how much insurance to put in place, but I can help you make that decision for yourself. There are two ways to think about how much insurance to put in place. The first is to focus on what you would like to be done if something did happen to you. I'll ask you some questions to make sure you're educated on some of the more important things you would like to cover. Based on what you tell me, I'll keep track of the amounts you think you'll need to make that happen and I can then give you premium pricing on the total cover that would be required to meet all your wishes. The other way to think about it is focusing on what you think you can afford to pay in premiums. You tell me how much you think you could pay each month and I can tell you how much cover you can get for that amount. The way I normally do this is to start with your wishes, let you know how much that would cost each month, and then if that's too much, we can work down towards a level of cover and cost that you feel good about. Will that work for you?"*

Experts in Life Insurance are Comfortable Discussing Death

People die. But very few people plan to die and actively seek out discussions around the consequences of their death. You need to be an expert in death and a professional when it comes to discussing death.

This is a very important point, but it's a difficult one on which to offer strategies. So often when I listen to calls and talk to advisors who can offer advice and sell face to face, there's an obvious level of discomfort talking about the death of the person that needs to be insured. I've heard everything from people who mumble the word "death" through to those who let out nervous giggles after they say the word during insurance conversations. Any habit or behaviour that suggests you're nervous about discussing someone's death is likely to damage your credibility.

There are a few things you can do. To make this conversation more comfortable, include the following:

1. **Go through the conversation yourself** – If you haven't discussed your own death, the impact that would have on others, your own wishes for what would happen and all other aspects of the insurance conversation, how can you expect to credibly engage someone else? If you think you're too young or have no needs in this area, have the conversation with a parent or relative. The more you understand and become emotionally

attuned to the consequences of death, the more committed and confident you'll be when the discussion happens.

2. **Start paying attention to death and aligning it to what you do** – Read the obituaries each day for a few weeks. The more your brain accepts that people really do die, the more comfortable you become with this concept. If you're reading the newspaper and see an article about a death from an accident or a murder, or some other story that includes people losing their lives, just stop and reflect. Spend some time thinking about those whom the person has left behind. Spend some time contemplating how much pain their family is going through and how that would be exacerbated by a lack of insurance.

3. **Develop skills around focusing death conversations on the partners of people you're discussing insurance with** – It's generally much easier for both you and the prospective customer to talk about how the death of the other person involved would impact their children, their finances and their quality of life. If you have this conversation first, it's often much easier to then transfer the discussion to discussing their own death.

Experts Behave like Experts

At 48 years of age, I am "old school" in a lot of my thinking. I still add punctuation to my texts, shave every workday, polish my shoes till they shine and stress when I'm one minute late for a meeting. I can appreciate that the world is changing. Standards and expectations are changing, and you would be justified in thinking some of the behaviours I'll outline are very "last century". From my perspective, I think all this change creates a great opportunity, especially for those of you who are new to your career in insurance. I believe that adopting "old school" behaviours will differentiate you from the rest and enable you to rapidly build credibility in an industry that requires a new level of respect and trust in society. Let's consider some of these behaviours:

1. **Be on time!** – Whether it's turning up to your place of business, an internal meeting or a customer call, it shouldn't make a difference. Failing to call or attend a meeting at the promised time sends a message to people that you probably can't be completely trusted when it comes to other aspects of the relationship. I certainly won't claim to be perfect in this area, but it is something I'm very conscious of and committed to.

2. **Be generous with your time** – The more you rush someone through their insurance purchasing journey, the more likely they are to feel like something's been missed. From a ROE (Return on Effort) perspective, you need to understand that doing the work will always result in a better return for both you and the customer. If you spend an extra two calls and an hour on the customer's insurance purchasing journey, I can almost guarantee that you will be paid back with much higher conversion rates and significantly lower cancellation rates. Solutions developed around needs rather than budget generally involve higher levels of cover, usually resulting in greater financial rewards for your efforts as well.

3. **Pay attention to your written communications** – Do your very best to eradicate spelling mistakes, poor grammar, poor formatting, confusing subject lines and a host of other lazy mistakes that make it look like you don't care. If people can't trust you with the detail, how can they possibly be confident that the policy you've put in place is the right one for them and the one they believe they've purchased? Once again, I'm not claiming perfection on this one, but when I send a written

communication, I go to great pains to ensure it presents me as a credible partner.

4. **Avoid complaining, blaming, criticising others (especially competitors)** – Avoid anything else that suggests you don't or won't take complete responsibility and accountability for anything that impacts the customer and their experience. I can appreciate that you can only control what you can control, but the customer really doesn't care who bears the fault.

All they care about is you taking responsibility for making their insurance purchasing journey as efficient, effective and enjoyable as possible.

We are our habits. Do your habits present you as a credible expert?

Experts Look
Like Experts

The way you dress each morning is a ritual that sends a message to your brain around who you plan to be when you get to work.

I can appreciate a lot of you reading this book will work in call centres and think it doesn't matter. It does. If you're more focused on looking like a rock star than you are on looking like a professional, you'll find it significantly more difficult to behave like a professional. Behaving like a professional involves doing the work, and that includes presenting yourself as a professional each day. If the people you work with give you a hard time for wearing a suit or a tie, remind yourself that 91 percent of performance payments go to less than 13 percent of insurance salespeople. If you want to break free of the 87 percent who fight over 9 percent of performance payments, stop dressing like they do.

Experts Sound
Like Experts

All the way through this book, I've been talking about the insurance conversation. A conversation with a sales professional is great, because the way they speak, ask questions, respond to questions and concerns and communicate in general is professional. I didn't grow up on the right side of town and have had to do a lot of work to sound more like a professional, and less like a kid who grew up on the beach and worked at McDonald's. (No disrespect to McDonald's – your system and what I learned working for you, has been a huge part of my success in life.)

When I started shooting video training in 2007, I was globally a very highly regarded (and paid) conference speaker. When I reviewed the videos we first shot, I was horrified to hear how colloquial I sounded. I'm proud of where I have come from, but sounding like the kid from the beach did not present me as credible. I committed to improving the way I speak at the age of 40, did hundreds of hours of speech exercises and deliberate work on the language I use. I had to work incredibly hard to change the communication habits and mannerisms I had built up over a lifetime. I often still sound like that kid from the beach, but when it's sales time, the new habits kick in. Most of the time, the way I communicate creates a perception of expertise, because the work I've done and continue to do has turned in to a better set of communication habits.

Doing the work includes committing to looking and sounding like a professional when you're engaged in your work life.

Experts Signal the Basis
of their Expertise

If you go back to the chapter on credible reasons, you'll understand that a huge part of this concept is about creating the perception of credibility early in an interaction. Effective delivery of a credible reason is even more important if you work in a call centre and make outbound calls or if you work in a bank branch and generate referrals to other specialists in your bank.

A lot of you will also be relatively young. Many of you won't have decades of experience in developing great insurance solutions and helping customers buy the right cover. That doesn't mean you can't easily and habitually create the perception of expertise. Talk about the thousands of claims your company has paid out on over the past year. Talk about the millions and billions of dollars of policies the company has put in place for people like the customer. Talk about the team you're surrounded by and the experience of those who support you in delivering insurance solutions.

I don't know you well enough to give you specific advice in this area, but I can tell you that it makes a difference. Start paying attention to what others in the team are doing. Talk about it in team meetings and when you review calls (if you're in a call centre). Pay attention to whether you're doing this effectively.

One thing I can recommend is avoiding talking about how great you or your company is before you've taken the time out to understand the customer and their needs. None of this matters until the prospective customer knows that you care about them and you can deliver something that may be of value to them.

Experts Have Fans
and References

Imagine being able to use this strategy to build credibility, reduce the probability of price shopping and differentiate yourself as an advisor.

BILL "When can I get back a quote with your recommendations?"

SALESPERSON *"I should be able to come back to you with recommendations and a proposed insurance solution next Thursday. I'm happy to do the work on that over the next week, but given that you've told me I'm competing against another advisor, there's something I need you to do between now and then. Are you OK with that?"*

BILL "It depends on what it is…"

SALESPERSON *"In a competitive situation, the hardest thing for me to prove is how good and how valuable my ongoing service is. So, I want you to ring one of three customers who are happy to take a call and share their experience. If I give you three names and phone numbers, can you promise to call one of them between now and when we meet to go through the solution?"*

Imagine them calling your existing customer. Hearing about how great you are. Hearing about how you call them every year to do the review and make sure their insurance matches their current situation. Imagine them telling the prospective customer how much better you are than the previous advisor they used. Imagine them selling how great you are to work with and telling the prospective customer they would be crazy to go with another advisor.

Do you think this would improve your conversion rate in competitive situations?

Imagine sending an email out to the three customers to let them know they may get a call. Having a credible reason to engage them and remind them they're a reference point for you and your business.

Imagine sending the person who gets the call a bottle of wine to say thanks for being such a great customer and supporter. Do you think they would go out of their way to refer you?

Even if the person you're selling to doesn't call them, you've still significantly differentiated yourself from any other advisor that doesn't proactively offer references to call.

If you sell service as part of your value proposition, and you're not engaging your happy customers in the sales process, you're missing a fantastic opportunity to build your credibility with very little effort on your part. If you're in a call centre and thinking,

"I can't use that strategy"

you're thinking too small. If you have a happy customer, there is the potential to make them a reference point.

Experts Convert More
and Get Paid More

Wow. That rant on the importance of deliberately building your credibility went a little longer than expected. This is such an important aspect of your ability to convert hard work into returns for you, the people you engage in insurance conversations with and the company you work for. Unfortunately, it's generally ignored, because insurance salespeople mistake high levels of rapport for high levels of trust.

You'll notice that often I was speaking more about what not to do than what to do. That's because most insurance salespeople need to focus more on not damaging their perceived credibility than they do on building it. Get rid of all the bad behaviours and you're way ahead of the average insurance salesperson. Replace them with credibility-building behaviours, and you're on your way to excellence and deserving to be part of the 13 percent who get paid 91 percent of performance payments above salary.

ARE YOU A LIKEABLE EXPERT?

Trust is a function of both rapport and credibility. Both must be in place for someone to trust you with the financial and mental wellbeing of their loved ones in the event of an insurance event. I want to share two last thoughts with you.

The first relates to the science of liking. I was lucky enough to be involved in a workshop with Dr Robert Cialdini in Arizona, where he spoke on the science of liking and what drives higher levels of rapport and liking between people. I was amazed at how much I had to learn on a topic I thought I knew quite a bit about. At the end of the presentation, he offered this pearl of wisdom: the primary driver of liking between you and another person is how much you like them.

Please pause and reflect on that. The more you like the other person, the more likely it is the two of you will be in a state of liking and you will receive all the benefits of achieving that mutual state.

A very important question you need to reflect on is

"How much do I genuinely like the people I assist in the insurance purchasing journey?"

Are you seeing them as targets to close a sale? Are you experiencing them as people you're forced to deal with? Are you hearing what they say and ask and you're thinking

"Why are these people so stupid?"

If you're smiling – stop it! You should be frowning. If you're having any of these thoughts and emotions, you're decreasing the probability that people will want you to help them in their insurance purchasing journey.

The second point I want to finish on, is the impact your subconscious intent has on your perceived credibility. People subconsciously know when your intent is to sell them something, make a quick buck or achieve anything self-centred. This is the opposite of customer centricity. I know in my heart and mind why I'm so passionate about the importance of helping people buy the right cover. Do you?

If this is something you're challenged by, I strongly recommend reading Simon Sinek's amazing book *Start With Why.*[11] Don't just check out the 20-minute TED talk. DO the work and read the book. Do the work and discover what drives your passion for working in the insurance industry. If you do the work and can't find a compelling reason to be in this industry, it's time to find another career. Trust is something you earn – and when you do the work, the rewards are amazing.

CHAPTER TEN

EXPLORING AND LISTENING

THE ANSWER IS IN THE QUESTION

The quality of the solutions you provide, the relationships you enjoy and the success or failure you experience, will be driven more by the quality of your questioning than any other sales skill.

I can appreciate that's a bold statement, but everything in my experience and the experience of literally thousands of sales leaders tells me that this is a truth. Organisations, compliance teams and quality assurance coaches set insurance salespeople up for failure by focusing more on the product features and benefits they want customers to be told about than the questions that need to be asked to establish relevance, value and a need that can be met. As an insurance professional, you cannot allow this to be an excuse. You must commit to translating everything you want to say into questions that can be asked.

To be truly committed to the customer-centric way, you must be committed to developing both your questioning and your listening skills. As Susan Scott noted in *Fierce Conversations*[12],

"The conversation is the relationship."

The more you fill your insurance conversations with great questions, the more you'll enjoy amazing customer relationships and support.

Once again, it would be easy to write an entire book on questions, and in many ways, I have. If you go back through the previous chapters and review all the examples I've provided, you'll see that in nearly every example script the focus is on the question that should be asked rather than the statement that should be made.

There are two things I want to achieve in this chapter. The first is to lock in some questioning wisdom. This is wisdom I've picked up over the last 30 years of my career that has radically changed the way I think about any conversation. While it's tempting to share our SIDE (Situation. Issues. Desires. Expectations) framework, I'm confident that developing a questioning framework using the PAVE Principle will set you up for success in developing great question plans for use in your insurance conversations. The second outcome I want to achieve is sharing some valuable strategies for listening more effectively. Failing to listen is at the core of dysfunctional and failed relationships. In my experience, listening is an art rarely practised at the level of good, let alone excellent.

SOME QUESTIONING WISDOM

I won't take credit for any of the wisdom I'm about to share. It's very difficult to attribute it to any one author, and all I can say is that I'm very grateful for learning many of these things early in my sales career. I have no doubt those of you who are highly experienced will be tempted to brush it aside with an,

"I already knew that"

and move on. Big mistake. I want to challenge you, especially to reflect on whether you're truly applying each piece of wisdom in every aspect of your insurance conversations.

Ask with Intent
to Learn

I didn't fill this book with scripts that highlight the questions you need to ask so that you could learn those questions. I did it to explain what it is you need to know about the people you're selling insurance to so that you can genuinely protect and provide for their loved ones. Without you knowing the answers to these questions, and the customer perceiving that you understand the answers to these questions, you'll fail to provide a truly customer-centric solution and experience.

The big point here is, if you're just going through the motions to ask for the information you need to achieve compliance, you've failed. You might make the sale, but you've failed the customer. To be frank, you've failed yourself. I often say that the most important aspect of sales – one that I can't teach, is genuine curiosity. To truly protect and provide you need to care about the customer's situation and turn up to every needs analysis as if it's the biggest event in your life. My pet hate is advisors that send out fact finds and expect customers to fill these out before they meet with them. I can appreciate that it's highly convenient for the Adviser, but I really don't buy into the value that advisors claim this creates for customers.

Disagree with this? Take some time out to reflect on it, and if you're keen for a debate, please let me know.

When You Ask a Question –
Shut Up and Listen

This is something I found very difficult early in my sales career. As you've probably picked up, I have some very strong opinions. It's also probably obvious that I'm very comfortable and happy to share them. The problem with this is that every moment you're speaking is a moment the customer is not sharing valuable information. As smart as you may be, helping a customer buy is much more about letting the customer find their way to a great solution than it is about you telling them what's right and what they need to do. This is the case whether you are licensed to provide advice or not.

The silence after you ask a question creates a wonderful moment. It creates time for the customer to consider, process and reflect on the answer from their perspective. It also creates a natural vacuum into which thoughts and feelings will flow, if you can just shut up long enough for the customer to speak and react in other less obvious ways. The more succinct your questions and the more space you create for answers, the more you'll learn and the better the customer will feel about sharing.

Never Accept the
First Answer

I'll attribute this piece of wisdom to David Maister and his co-authors in the groundbreaking book, *The Trusted Advisor*[13]. This is a must-read for any professional in the insurance industry, whether you're currently licensed to provide advice or not. The concept is simple and yet so powerful. What Maister suggests is that when a person you're speaking to answers a question, you must always ask further questions to develop a deeper understanding of their answer. Let me share an example.

SALESPERSON *"Bill, who are the people you want to protect and provide for with the insurance you're considering?"*

BILL "My wife and kids."

The average salesperson gets on with the fact find and rushes towards the sale. The professional insurance salesperson knows they can't accept the first answer and must dig deeper.

SALESPERSON *"Great. And how old are the children?"*

BILL "Mary is 13 and Billy is 9."

SALESPERSON *"Thanks, Bill. How is Mary finding high school?"*

BILL "Really good. She goes to Girls' Grammar, and she's finding the sports program really good there. She seems to be doing OK, considering she's just hit her teenage years."

SALESPERSON *"That's always good to hear. I was perfect as a teenager, but my sister was a terror. And, how did you choose Grammar?"*

BILL "There were a few other schools in the area, but we were keen to give her the best shot at school that we could, and the teachers there are great. It costs a fortune, but she's worth it."

As you can see, by asking a few deeper questions, there is so much you can learn about the customer, their situation and their motivation for wanting to purchase insurance. As we learned in the PAVE Principle, this understanding will enable us to create a higher level of perceived value when we present our solution. It should also trigger off a note to find out if school fees are something Bill would want to be covered in his insurance solution and we can come back to that later in our insurance conversation when we're helping him quantify how much cover he thinks he needs.

The Person Asking the Question is in Control of the Conversation

The more certain a customer feels that the solution is right, the more likely they are to act and purchase cover. The clearer it is that you're following a proven process for helping them define their needs, the more certain they'll feel. What this means is that the more you control the process, the more confident they will feel about you and the solution you help them develop.

If you try to control a conversation by telling people what's next, you'll rarely create a customer-centric experience for the customer. And, they're more likely to feel like they're being sold to. If you guide a conversation with questions, you'll maintain control and make the customer feel like you're educating them and helping them to buy. Here's an example of how you can subtly and ethically use questions to control the direction of the conversation.

SALESPERSON *"Joan, if something happened to you and your income was no longer available, what would you want to happen to the family home?"*

JOAN "What do you mean?"

SALESPERSON *"Well. There's generally three options. The family could sell the home, but obviously, they would need somewhere else to live. If there's enough cash in the bank, they could pay out the mortgage. Or, if there is insurance in place, that could be used to pay out the mortgage. What would be your preference?"*

JOAN "I definitely don't have that much cash available. I guess I would want the insurance to pay it out."

SALESPERSON *"OK, Joan. How much insurance would you need to pay out the entire mortgage?"*

JOAN "About $400,000."

SALESPERSON *"Great. That's an amount you may want to insure. Outside of needing somewhere to live, have you thought about how much the living expenses would be to keep the family running each year?"*

As you can see from this example, the insurance sales professional effortlessly guides the conversation from debt to living expenses by using questions. This may be something Joan has never thought about, and the question educates her without giving advice. The big point is that you can help the customer buy AND maintain control of the conversation.

The Best Way to Provoke an Issue is With a Question

I can accept that it might be faster to just say something like this:

SALESPERSON *"Look Joan. If you died, from what you've told me, your husband's income wouldn't support the mortgage, and he would probably have to sell the family home. On top of that, there are living expenses he would need to find to feed the kids and pay their school fees. So, if you want them to keep the home, stay in the schools they're currently at, and afford to eat for the next three years, you'll need about $700,000 of insurance."*

I hope by now you know that I would not recommend this.

As you can see from the previous example, asking great questions to help the customer educate themselves on the problems their loved ones face is a far more customer-centric way to engage in the insurance conversation. The more you make problem statements, the more defensive the person you're speaking to is likely to become. The more you help them understand problems by asking great questions, the more likely they are to be mentally and emotionally invested in solving those problems with you.

Questions are the Best Response to an Objection

So much time is wasted developing self-serving, impractical objection responses and force-feeding these to salespeople, who are then coached to force feed them to customers with concerns. This is not the customer-centric way. When a person providing an objection (generally a concern) is responded to with a genuine question, the pressure shifts from the salesperson to the person providing the concern. Here's an example:

BILL "I just don't think I can afford that much per month."

SALESPERSON *"Thanks for letting me know that Bill. I can appreciate that's probably more than you had hoped to pay. What part of the risk do you think you can comfortably not pay for? We've talked about the mortgage on the house, the debt on the car, the living expenses of $65,000 per annum for 3 years and the kids' school fees. Is there one of those you would feel comfortable taking out of the cover?"*

If You're Asking Questions,
the Customer is Giving Themselves Advice

One final point I want to make here can be a contentious one. Please do not take this as advice, and consult your compliance team on their position on this. My opinion and belief is, if you're asking questions, you are not providing advice. This is an incredibly valuable distinction for those of you who are operating under a limited/no advice or general advice licence.

When you realise this and your organisation buys into it, you can go to work on creating questioning strategies for all those moments in the conversation when you wish you could just tell a customer what to do.

THE LOST
ART OF LISTENING

It happened a long time before the internet, text messages and Gen Y, so I'm not going to blame any of those for the diabolical lack of listening I commonly observe when reviewing phone and face-to-face insurance conversations.

If you want to radically increase the probability of a noncompliant call, it's easy. Just fail to listen and sell the customer a solution that doesn't match their stated needs. I say that with an element of seriousness, because of the number of compliance breaches, complaints and claims arguments that could have all been avoided had the salesperson just practised the "two ears, one mouth" philosophy of communication.

To listen – and want to listen, is at the core of the customer-centric way.

Like any other skill, listening needs to be taught, practised, reviewed, reflected upon and coached if you truly want this skill to be a differentiator in the way you help customers buy the right cover.

Let's start with a few thoughts on some common mistakes and their causes.

COMMON LISTENING CRIMES AGAINST CUSTOMERS

It is very difficult to observe your own listening failures.

My strong suggestion is that you spend time listening to other people's calls and observe other advisors' face-to-face meetings with a singular focus on looking and listening for these common mistakes. The more you observe them, the more you'll train your brain to avoid them.

The number one cause of a failure to listen is a failure to remain "in the moment". If you're busy booting up the system, looking at emails, thinking about your lunch break or next meeting, or your mind is on anything but what the customer is saying, you're probably engaging in "Listening Crimes". I appreciate that "crimes" is very strong language, but I've used it deliberately.

If you're committed to customer centricity, you need to see poor listening as a crime against the people who are trusting you with their insurance purchasing journey. The insurance purchasing journey is a complex one for the average customer and, whether you're providing advice or not, they're relying on you and your undivided attention.

Crime #1
Rushing the Sale

When we're in a rush to achieve any outcome, the brain responds by focusing only on things that will speed up our progress towards that outcome. If all you're focused on is the sale, you miss things like the names of the person's partner or children, the emotion in the prospective customer's voice, the motivation behind the customer's interest in the insurance conversation and a host of other things that turn the sale into a valuable conversation. The more you remind yourself that your primary role is to help the customer understand their needs and buy the right cover, the less likely it becomes that rushing will reduce listening.

Crime #2
Talking Over the Customer

I cringe every time I hear this happen in a call or watch it happen in a meeting. And unfortunately, this means I cringe a lot! As a rule, if the customer is speaking, wait until there is a slightly uncomfortable pause before you start speaking or ask the next question. If you listen for this pause, it will dramatically improve your listening and your connection to what the customer is saying.

Crime #3
Making Hasty Judgements

I hear this a lot when people are carrying out the underwriting part of the customer's insurance journey. The customer answers a question in a manner that suggests there could be an issue and one of two things happen. The insurance sales professional only listens to details that enable them to tick the necessary boxes and get past that part of the underwriting process. This is obviously not protecting the organisation you work for, and it is very likely to cause great harm at a later and critical date. Or the opposite happens, the insurance professional makes a rash judgement that the person will never be insured, fails to ask for further detail and rushes to get the underwriting process over and done with. This often results in the insured missing out on the cover that could have been achieved. Both behaviours fail the protect and provide test.

Crime #4
Avoiding and Omitting
Premium Reducing Facts
and Circumstances

While most people do not have adequate cover, many people can carry on a good life without covering every risk that would increase their insurance cover. As a simple example, many partners could pay off a smaller mortgage with the salary they earn. So, it may not be necessary to cover the entire mortgage. Failing to ask about this, or pose the option to a customer for consideration, is unlikely to be noncompliant. Having said that, this doesn't mean it's ethical. It also means you've missed a great opportunity to build your credibility and overtly display your customer centricity.

AVOIDING
LISTENING CRIMES

Arguably, the title of this section should be improving listening and customer connection. But with what I've observed across 25 countries and countless companies, avoiding bad listening habits is what I want you to use as motivation for improving your listening skills. It's more motivating to commit to not being a poor listener, than it is to become a great listener.

I'm hoping that when you review your calls or receive feedback on your meetings, you find out you're already using many of these skills, and they're a natural part of your communication habits. Please don't just read through these and leave it at that. Commit to coming back to this list and constantly considering and seeking feedback on whether you're regularly using active and reflective listening skills.

Listening Skill #1
Encouragers

The average prospective customer rarely understands just how much information you need to do your job effectively. Most people buying insurance for the first time weren't thinking about their personal health and risk profile before they called you or you reached out to them. To help people provide you with more information, one of the active listening strategies you can use is "encouragers". An encourager is a word or sound that signals the customer is on track and confirms you're listening to what they're saying. Examples are words and phrases like *"OK"*, *"wow"*, *"mm-hmm"* and *"that's interesting"*. The more you use encouragers (within reason), the more confident the customer will be that you're listening and the more information they will share.

Listening Skill #2
Door Openers

The next level of encourager is a "door opener". This is a word or phrase that clearly signals to the customer that more information is desired and required. These cause the customer to share more detail and often yield incredibly valuable information that otherwise may have been missed. Imagine that a customer has just told you,

"Well, something came up on the brain scan, but the doctor said it was nothing."

A door opener to encourage them to provide further detail might be something as simple as,

"OK,"

(delivered in a concerned/questioning tone) or a statement:

"Wow, that must have been a relief!"

(followed by a pause/silence) or an actual question:

"Wow, that must have been a relief. Did they give you any more detail?"

(in a concerned tone)

Listening Skill #3
Emotional Descriptors

Just because you've heard the words, doesn't mean you've heard what the customer was saying. People's tone, language, pace and volume can all radically change the meaning of the same set of words. When you use an emotional descriptor like,

"It sounds like you're pretty concerned about that?"

a few important things happen. The first is that you challenge yourself to listen more intently. To hear and describe someone's emotion requires you to switch on your listening in a much more active and focused manner. The second is that you send a signal to the customer that you've invested enough in the conversation to be listening to much more than just the answers you need to give them a price. It's also a great test of your comprehension of what's been said and avoids assumptions on what the customer is trying to convey.

Listening Skill #4
Recycling Names and Information

If a customer provides you with the name of their partner or their children, they've shared something that's incredibly important to them. Challenge yourself to recycle this valuable information by using it in a following statement or question. Asking,

"Is James working?"

after Jenny has told you her partner's name, is far more connected than asking,

"Does your partner work?"

The same goes for things like where the children go to school, where the house is, how much income they earn and any other key aspect of their life that impacts the cover they may require.

Listening Skill #5
Defining and Exploring Key Words

A great strategy for increasing your focus and listening actively, is listening for key words in the customer's response. Let me share an example of this.

> **BILL** "The insurance is to cover the wife and kids in case anything happens to me."

> **SALESPERSON** *"Thanks, Bill. How long have you and the wife been together?"*

> **BILL** "10 years next May."

SALESPERSON *"Next May. Fantastic. And congratulations. What's her name?"*

BILL "Jenny."

SALESPERSON *"Great. And is Jenny working, or is she looking after the children full time?"*

BILL "She's at home for the moment."

SALESPERSON *"OK. Great. And are you renting the home or have you bought a place?"*

If you read back through this interaction, you'll notice that every question includes a reference to a keyword used in the previous statement. Challenging yourself to leverage this strategy makes you listen more actively, improves the flow of the conversation and makes it easier for the other person to share information.

Listening Skill #6
Attentive Silence

As I mentioned before, silence creates a vacuum into which valuable customer information will often flow. When the customer knows that you're listening in an attentive manner, they become more likely to keep sharing information. When you use encouragers or door openers with attentive silence, you'll be very surprised at how much more information gets shared and how much more of it you hear. This also helps you avoid talking over the customer.

Listening Strategy #7
Paraphrasing

Paraphrasing is simply repeating words that the customer has used, to confirm that you've heard what they've said. Once again, this generally promotes further sharing of information and signals that you hear what has been said. Here's an example of effective paraphrasing.

> **BILL** "Yeah, I've been putting it off because it all seemed too hard and I've been so busy."

> **SALESPERSON** *"Sure, Bill. I can appreciate that you've been so busy with everything else, that's meant you haven't had time to get the insurance in place for the family. That's why I gave you a call, so that we can take this off your 'to do' list. Can I just ask..."*

SEEK TO UNDERSTAND BEFORE SEEKING TO BE UNDERSTOOD

As I mentioned in the previous chapter, this is a piece of wisdom from Stephen Covey that you need to make a part of the way you sell insurance and help customers buy the right cover. Effective and customer-centric questioning will improve your understanding, build rapport and create a perception of higher credibility and expertise. That's a great return for a little bit of extra, and very important work. Great questioning is only truly customer centric when it's coupled with great listening. Listening is not necessarily hearing, and you need to commit to excellence in demonstrating that you not only have two ears and one mouth but also know how to use them in that ratio.

The understanding you'll develop from this skill will set you up to either recommend or provide pricing (if you can't provide advice) on the right cover. It will help you avoid budget-focused sales practices and still leave the door open to offer a more limited cover solution, if affordability is a genuine issue.

For most, what follows needs analysis is offering or presenting a solution. But before we go there, I want to suggest there's an in-between step that differentiates between those who sell insurance and those who help customers buy the right cover.

CHAPTER ELEVEN

GAINING PERMISSION

DO YOU HAVE PERMISSION TO OFFER A SOLUTION?

It is a waste of your energy and time trying to sell to someone who's not ready to buy.

Some great wisdom I got early in my career was that there are three questions you need a prospective customer to answer in securing a new sale. The most important part of the advice was that the order of the questions is incredibly important and that there is no point in exerting energy on the second or third question until the first has been answered. The three questions in order were:

1. Why do/buy anything?

2. Why buy yours/from you?

3. Why buy now?

Reflect on these three questions and consider how much time you spend in your sales process on each of the questions? As an example, do you rush to tell people how great your company is before you've confirmed they're in the market? Do you try to close a sale before you've confirmed they're committed to improving or putting in place their insurance cover? These are very common mistakes and signals that you're not selling in a customer-centric manner – signals that you're more committed to selling something than you are to helping the person buy the right cover.

The customer-centric insurance salesperson is totally focused on educating a customer on how to assess their current situation and highlighting the potential insurance needs that may or may not flow from that situation. If you maintain a focus on this, you won't jump ahead and try to sell the customer on "Why buy yours/ from you?" or "Why buy now?" until they've confirmed they're ready to buy something. I refer to this as "gaining permission" to offer a solution. Underestimate the importance of this small step at your own peril!

The customer-centric insurance salesperson only moves into offering solutions (including pricing) and sharing options once a clear need has been established.

MAGIC HAPPENS WHEN YOU GAIN PERMISSION

If you've executed the PAVE process effectively and the customer has a genuine need, they will be absolutely primed to act. This is an exciting moment in the sales process for you. You experience a level of confidence that your hard work is about to turn into a new customer. You also experience a sense of achievement in helping a person understand their situation and the need for smarter cover choices. But this is often where rushing to the sale damages the customer's level of comfort and your perceived credibility.

Let's consider an example where the insurance salesperson is rushing to the sale and doesn't gain permission. This is the standard in the industry and while it's compliant and ethical, a major opportunity to improve the relationship with the customer is missed.

> **BILL** "Yeah. That amount of insurance seems about right. I am really keen to make sure there's no debt left on the house if something happens and I hadn't thought about living expenses and Mary needing to get a job to pay the bills."

> **SALESPERSON** *"Great, Bill. So, that totals $647,000. How about I give you a quote for that much life insurance and also give you a quote for $700,000 just to provide a round number and a little extra comfort money for Mary and the kids?"*

> **BILL** "Sure."

Most of you will be a little confused right now. Everything in this example seems fine. The insurance salesperson has turned a confirmed need into an opportunity and is about to provide pricing. What's the problem?

Smart insurance salespeople know that once they've helped the customer establish a clear need and answered,

"Why do/buy anything?"

they need to gain permission before they launch into helping them answer

"Why buy ours/from me?"

and

"Why buy now?"

As you read the example I'm about to provide, really think through what's happening to the dynamic between Bill and the insurance person. Take a little time out and visualise this conversation in your mind and try to experience it from Bill's perspective rather than yours. Gaining permission goes something like this:

BILL "Yeah. That amount of insurance seems about right. I am really keen to make sure there's no debt left on the house if something happens and I hadn't thought about living expenses and Mary needing to get a job to pay the bills."

SALESPERSON *"Great, Bill. We've been through a discussion about debt, living expenses and the opportunity to leave behind a legacy. In relation to the debt on the house and the living expenses, we discussed before, the total amount was $647,000. Do you think there's anything else you need to consider in relation to what you might want to cover with insurance?"*

BILL "Not really. I think that about covers it."

SALESPERSON *"Thanks, Bill. Would you like me to let you know what the options are for putting that sort of cover in place and what health questions and checks might be required?"*

BILL "Sure. That would be great."

What's the difference? If you didn't pick it up, please reread the example and spend a little more time considering this.

In both examples, Bill confirmed that he had a problem. He confirmed that the insurance salesperson had helped him define that problem more effectively. (He hadn't previously thought about living expenses). In both examples, the insurance salesperson helped Bill quantify that problem into an amount he might want to think about covering. Excellent work and all very customer centric and compliant.

The big difference is that in the second example the insurance salesperson didn't assume that just because Bill confirmed he has a problem, that they have permission to solve it.

If you're challenged by this concept think about how annoying it is when you share a problem with a friend or partner, and they go straight into problem-solving mode. Instead of asking how you feel about the problem, they tell you what you should be doing and how to fix it. Just because you shared a problem with them, doesn't mean you gave them permission to fix it! And it's the same with a prospective customer. Just because they have a problem and a confirmed need, doesn't mean that they gave you permission to sell them the solution.

By confirming the problem and spending an extra 15 seconds gaining permission to offer a solution, we move from someone trying to sell them something to a professional who has been given permission to help them buy a solution. It's a subtle difference, but if you put this into practice, you'll notice a very different dynamic as you move into offering solutions and options. The prospective customer will be more engaged, more cooperative and more likely to give you valuable and honest feedback on how they feel about the options available.

Importantly, if they're not ready to buy, they're likely to share that with you before you launch into trying to sell them something.

HOW DO I KNOW IF THEY'RE READY TO BUY?

The easy answer to this question is "when they tell you they want a solution". If you master the art of seeking permission before you try to sell people a solution, they will generally let you know how ready they are at that point. And yet so often, even when we've gained permission to offer a solution, people fail to make decisions and take the action both you and they know needs to be taken.

This generally happens because we've failed to gain four important commitments along the way. Gaining these commitments along the way causes the prospective customer to answer,

"Why buy ours/from me?"

and

"Why buy now?"

at a subconscious level. It also makes it much less likely that putting the right cover in place will be derailed following the presentation of a solution that meets and matches their stated needs.

If you fail to achieve these four commitments, you'll experience a lot more stalled sales and cover opportunities. If you sell insurance over the phone, presenting a solution and confirming eligibility for someone that has no intention of buying or deciding probably wastes about 30 minutes to an hour of your time. It's not the end of the world, but it is frustrating. For most of you selling over the phone, you can probably justify this as a trade-off against the increased probability of a sale that going through the underwriting process creates.

If you provide advice and sell insurance face-to-face, you need to be more deliberate about achieving these commitments before you agree to go back to the office and work on a solution. Doing all the work to create and document a solution for someone who's not ready to buy could waste half a day or more. That's a very expensive mistake, and it takes you away from speaking to people who are serious about covering their risks and from doing existing customer reviews.

Apart from the time wasted, this also drains your energy. Selling to people who aren't ready to buy is painful. It leaves your pipeline full of unresolved opportunities. More importantly, it leaves the world full of underinsured people who are "thinking about it" or shopping around in an underinsured state. Neither is ideal.

The four "commitment tests" you can use, to assess how ready someone is to buy from you, can be remembered by using the acronym IDEA.

THE IDEA MODEL

Imagine you are just about to put effort into preparing or presenting a solution and taking someone through the underwriting process. Before you start using your time to do that, I jump out from behind a pot plant and yell,

"Do you really have any IDEA if this person is ready to buy, buy from you and buy now?"

I can appreciate this is probably a scary thought.

I hope if you're a manager, you'll seriously think about making this one of your coaching rituals.

What's "scary" for me is you wasting your time and your energy. What's scary for me is how many people are happy to use up an insurance salesperson's time, experience and expertise in

DEAN MANNIX | PROTECT AND PROVIDE

helping them buy the right solution with no intent of paying them back with their custom. Selling to people who are not ready to buy can be avoided if you ask these four questions and answer them honestly.

Intention to Cover?

Does the person I'm selling to have an intention to buy?

The "I" in the IDEA Model stands for "Intent". If you go back through all the stalled opportunities in your pipeline, you'll generally find that it is very difficult to honestly come up with something the customer did or said that provided clear evidence they were serious about acting to put the right cover in place. If you've confirmed a need, but your gut is telling you the person is unlikely to act, you need to test that before you put in more effort.

Here are a few examples of how you might do that. (Other than the Gaining Permission strategy I shared above)

SALESPERSON *"Great, Bill. We've been through a discussion about debt, living expenses and the opportunity to leave behind a legacy. In relation to the debt on the house and the living expenses we discussed before, the total amount was $647,000. Do you think there's anything else you need to consider in relation to what you might want to cover with insurance?"*

BILL "Not really. I think that about covers it."

SALESPERSON *"Great, Bill. I'm keen to offer you a solution to cover all of that, but I'm just keen to check in on where you're at. How important is it for you to cover those risks?"*

OR

> *"Great, Bill. Can I just check in before we go any further? Is there anything that's likely to make it hard for you to put that sort of cover in place?"*

OR

> *"Great Bill. I can give you a high-level monthly premium estimate on that level of policy. But because it's over $500,000, it's important that you understand I can't confirm an exact price until we go through some more detailed health questions. That could take us a while. Are you OK with that?"*

I know that some of you, including all the managers and coaches reading this, might be saying,

"Are you crazy? There's a live opportunity on the line, and this could scare them off before I get an opportunity to close them."

I can appreciate this view. I have no doubt many of you think that your amazing closing and objection handling skills will be enough to get them across the line. I can appreciate that many of you think it's better to close hard and worry about the attempt to cancel later. I get all that, and I respect your right to make the call on how you approach these types of situations.

For me personally, I would far prefer to find out that the person has concerns or a lack of intent before I do the work on developing a solution, offering a solution and potentially even going through a more detailed underwriting policy.

Make sure you're testing this before doing too much of the work. My recommendation is that you confirm this if you're having doubts or think the person is just going through the process to be polite or price up something they have no intent of purchasing from you.

Defined Decision-Making Process

Do you have a clear understanding of the prospective customer's decision-making strategy?

The "D" in the IDEA Model is for "Decision". Smart insurance professionals are making sure that, as they help the customer through their insurance purchasing journey, they're seeking to understand the person's decision-making process.

If you're selling over the phone, here is an all-too-common example of what often happens when you fail to understand and build commitments around the person's decision-making process.

SALESPERSON *"Great news, Bill. The underwriting process is complete, the cover you wanted to put in place is available, and all we need to do now is confirm that you're happy for me to put that in place for you. "You'll be covered straight away, subject to the exclusions we've discussed. Shall we go through the confirmation process?"*

BILL "Just send me all the paperwork and I'll have a look through it in more detail. I just need to run it past my accountant before I commit to anything."

Let me make something abundantly clear here. I have no issue with someone leveraging trusted advisors like their accountant to help them with important financial decisions. Often that's a smart thing to do. But we all know that often this is an excuse rather than a genuine desire to seek outside counsel. We also know that the person is unlikely to see their accountant in a hurry – and importantly, we know the person is uninsured or underinsured while they wait to see their accountant. If you had known they needed to see their accountant, you could have helped them by giving them the opportunity to see their accountant before you went through the underwriting process. That would have saved you a lot of time and given you a reason to follow them up. We could have avoided this – or at the very least put ourselves in a much better position to handle it, if we had sought commitment on their decision-making process before we offered a solution. This might have been achieved by making the following part of the conversation, before offering a solution:

SALESPERSON *"Great, Mary. We've been through a discussion about debt, living expenses and the opportunity to leave behind a legacy. In relation to the debt on the house and the living expenses we discussed before, the total amount was $647,000. Do you think there's anything else you need to consider in relation to what you might want to cover with insurance?"*

MARY "Not really. I think that about covers it."

SALESPERSON *"Thanks, Mary. I'm keen to offer you a solution to cover all of that, and I'm keen to know how much detail you need. Is there anyone else you need to run this by before you put the cover in place?"*

MARY "Yeah. I'll need to run it by my husband, Bill."

SALESPERSON *"That makes sense, Mary. How do you think he'll feel about the amount of cover we've discussed and having living expenses covered above the cost of paying out the mortgage?"*

MARY "Pretty good."

SALESPERSON *"That's good to hear. Are there any specific concerns he's likely to have about the amount of cover we've discussed?"*

MARY "No. I think that all makes sense."

SALESPERSON *"OK, great. Some people's partners like to see all the detail and others just want to be involved in the decision... Other than the premium amount each month, is there much other detail you'll need to share with him to make a decision and get the cover in place?"*

MARY "Not really. He'll just want to make sure we can budget for the payments."

SALESPERSON *"Great. What I can do now is give you an estimate of the premium. That will enable you to have the discussion with Bill and figure out the budgeting side of things. Do you think you'll talk that through tonight?"*

MARY "Probably."

SALESPERSON *"OK. I'll get an estimate of the premium from the system now. I'll also send you through an email with the exclusions we discussed, so you have those in writing. What we can do is book in a time for tomorrow to speak and that will give you time to speak to Bill. If the two of you are comfortable you can budget for the premium, we can go through all the health questions tomorrow and then I can confirm an exact amount. But if you think the premium is too much for the budget, then tomorrow you can tell me what you both think you can afford and I can let you know how much cover can*

> *be provided for that amount of monthly premium.*
> *Either way we can get insurance in place for you*
> *tomorrow, to make sure you're covered. Does that*
> *work for you, Mary?"*

I know this seems like extra effort, but think through how much easier it will be to get a decision tomorrow. Think about how much better Mary will feel about making that decision and how much more supportive Bill will be. And think through what you've just done to the probability of achieving a decision and cover in tomorrow's call.

The more you understand a person's decision-making process, the more commitment you can build into a decision and the easier it will be to ensure that confirmed needs are turned into covered customers.

Shared Expectations

Have you achieved shared expectations on what will be required to successfully put in place and pay for the right insurance solution?

The "E" in the IDEA Model stands for "Expectations". The more two people share the same expectations before a solution is presented, the more likely it is that decisions and agreements will be achieved when the solution is presented. This level of commitment is not as important for someone selling insurance on the phone, but here's an example of how you might build up a commitment to expectations:

SALESPERSON *"Mary. I'll put all of that into the system so I can give you an estimate of the monthly premium to cover the $647,000 we've been talking about. Can I just ask, are you comfortable with fitting the premium payments into your budget?"*

OR

"Bill. Do you think Mary will support you on adding an extra $120 a month on to the premiums to provide that extra $100,000 for the children's school fees?"

OR

"Bill. We've obviously been focused on what risks you might consider covering and how much insurance it would take to pay out debts like the home mortgage. But something I probably should have asked is whether you had an amount in mind that you think you can fit into the budget to cover all these risks. How much do you think you can afford each month to make sure the cover is in place?"

Where you set up common expectations before you present a final solution, there's a lot less thinking to be done, because you've had the discussion about these sorts of things before you offered the solution. This makes it much easier to achieve an agreement and much easier for the prospective customer to decide and put the cover in place.

Where you're offering advice and helping people buy larger policies, this is even more important. The less you surprise someone with things like the cost of the premiums, the rigour of the health checks, any potential exclusions and the amount of financial information they may have to provide, the more likely it is they'll be able to decide. If you surprise someone when you present a solution because they expected something very different, it makes it much harder for them to decide immediately. And as we know, when they leave your office without deciding, they're back on the street and not covered.

Access to Information and Joint Decision Makers

Do you have access to the required information and decision makers?

The "A" in the IDEA Model is for "Access". The level of access you've provided to others involved in the decision, and a person's willingness to provide the information you need, tells you a lot about how serious they are about placing the cover with you.

This becomes highly relevant if you offer advice and structure more complex solutions for business partners and people with complex financial situations. If you know you're likely to need this sort of information later in the purchasing journey, let the person you're dealing with know that early in the process. If you set that access expectation and they send you signals it will be difficult, make sure you explore their concerns and decide about how much effort you're willing to contribute to developing a solution for them.

MAKE SURE YOU'RE TREATED FAIRLY

We live in a world where people are told every day that they should shop around and negotiate aggressively with financial services companies like banks and insurance companies. An unfortunate side effect of this is that many people have lost respect for the value (and cost) of your time.

For most of you, your financial success in life will be dramatically impacted by how effectively you use your time. The more time you spend helping people who are genuinely interested in buying cover and value your help, the more successful you'll be. You need to make sure you spend most of your time with people who will value your efforts and are willing to reward you with their business and ongoing loyalty.

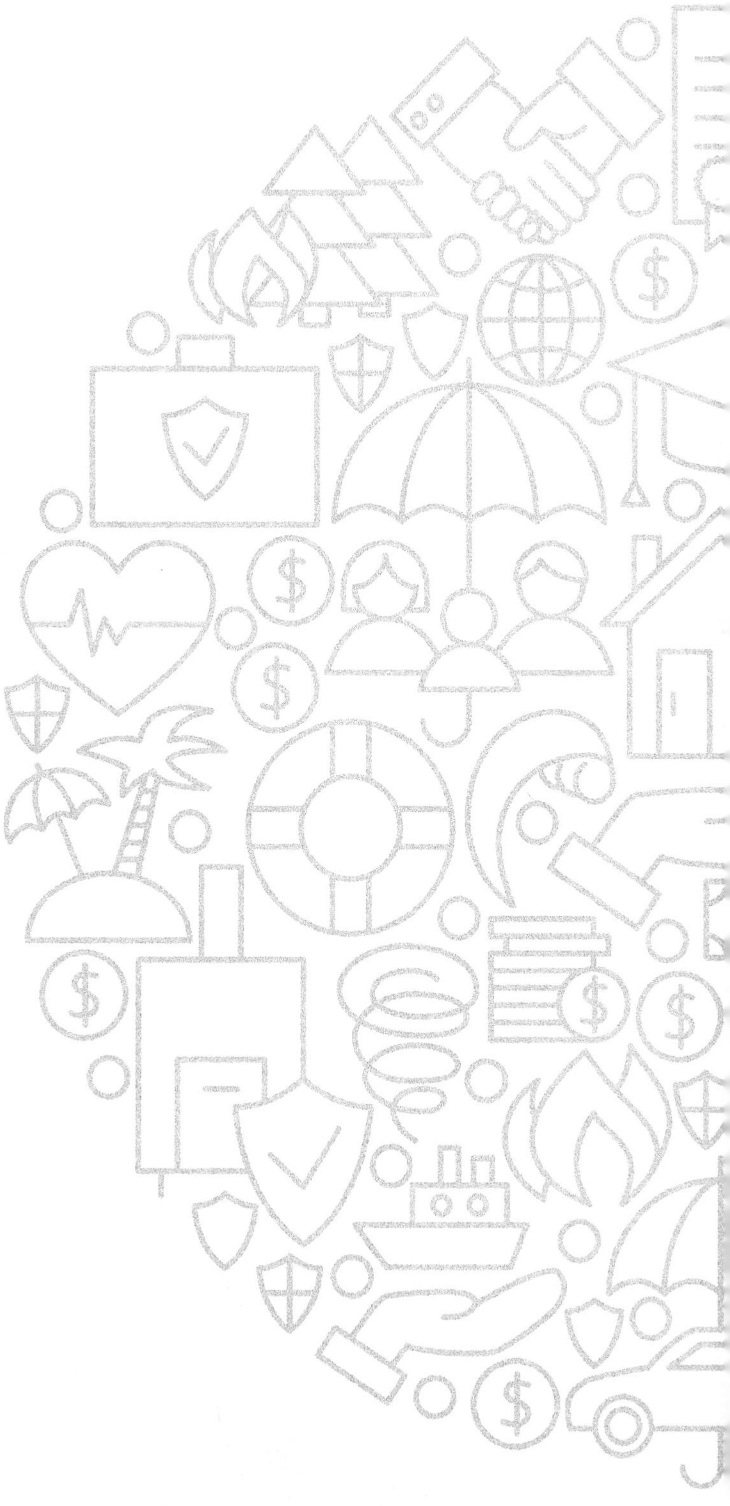

CHAPTER TWELVE

OFFERING SOLUTIONS

CONFIRMING
IS BETTER
THAN OFFERING

Customer-centric salespeople don't make sales. They earn them.

Can you believe it? We are over 50,000 words into a book on selling, and we're finally talking about offering a solution! Some of you might be asking,

"Does this crazy guy really want me to do all that work before I present my solution? When do we get to the close?"

Here's the great news. If you've "done the work" and taken the prospective customer through their insurance purchasing journey the way I'm asking you to, you've already made the sale. You're confirming a solution, rather than offering one because all the hard work you've done has led someone to answer all three questions I talked about in the previous chapter. Their state of mind will be:

"I understand why I need to put the right cover in place. There is clearly a problem I need to solve. You've delivered fantastic value in helping me define that problem and understanding how I can use life insurance to solve it. I like dealing with you, and I want you to take care of this for me. This is not going to go away, and if I fail to decide and act, I'll be walking the street uncovered or underinsured and putting the welfare of those I love at risk. And I know I need to do it now."

Yes, you had to do a lot of work to get here. But that work has earned you the sale. Now you just need to collect it!

COLLECTING THE SALE WITH ETHICAL INFLUENCE

I've talked a lot about the work of Dr Robert Cialdini in this book. Something you need to know about and explore is the body of influence research out there on what makes people more likely to say,

"Yes"

in sales situations. There's also a similar amount of research on things salespeople do that make it more likely for people to say,

"No"

in sales situations. In my work over the past 20 years, I've found that removing the behaviours that cause the "no's" has a far greater and immediate impact on sales, when compared to introducing the behaviours associated with higher levels of agreement. Please reread what I've just said. It's incredibly important because what I'm telling you is that you'll make more sales if you can remove a few bad behaviours.

The challenge is that you're probably unaware of what those bad behaviours are because most of the people around you are doing the same things. Even worse, you may have been coached to do them.

I've done my best to highlight many of these bad behaviours throughout this book and offer you alternatives that are aligned to what the research tells us is more likely to be successful. You'll need to do the work in figuring out what changes and improvements you need to make because I can't observe you personally. I have NEVER listened to a call or sat with an advisor and observed a solution presentation that couldn't be improved.

What I want to share with you in this chapter is how to use ethical influence strategies during your solution presentation.

The consistent and disciplined use of these strategies will increase the probability that all the hard work you've done translates into a sale for you and the right cover for the customer.

"From" is More
Important Than "To"

People don't buy solutions. They choose to solve a problem.

If you've engaged in a truly customer-centric conversation, you've covered a lot of ground and collected a lot of information from the prospective customer. Even the person that came to you just asking for a price has been challenged around whether the amount of insurance they asked for is genuinely going to meet their needs. If you provide advice in face-to-face situations, you probably had to go away and do quite a bit of work to develop the solution. If you're selling insurance over the phone, you've probably been engaging the customer for at least 10 to 15 minutes, and their attention span (and probably yours) is being stretched.

I'll assume you've executed the relevant strategies to make sure you've gained permission effectively and the customer wants you to offer some ideas on how to solve their problems.

Now, before you move into telling a customer what the solution is (including the premium cost), take a breath, slow things down, and remind them of the problems the solution is going to solve.

This primes the brain to perceive that there is greater value in the solution and greater urgency in putting the solution into place. It reconnects you with the customer and reminds them that you're on the insurance purchasing journey together. It sends an overt signal that you've been listening to what they've said and you truly understand their needs. Effectively engaging in this would sound something like the following:

SALESPERSON *"Great, Bill. Before I offer some ideas on how we could insure all the risks we discussed, I'm keen to quickly summarise my understanding. Is that OK?"*

BILL "Sure."

SALESPERSON *"Thanks, Bill. My understanding is that taking care of the family is what's important to you. You and Mary have been married eight years. You have two children, and Billy is eight and Jenny is nine. They both go to the local school. Your plan is for them to go to private high schools and you figure that's going to cost at least $150,000 for each of them. Mary isn't working and looks after* *the children, but she's probably going to head back to part-time at a local medical practice where she would be a General Practitioner and earn about $110,000 a year for the three days a week she wants to work. So, if something was to happen to you, Mary has earning capacity. The living expenses you thought she would need to get the kids through high school over the next 10 years were an extra $50,000 a year, so that totalled $500,000. The mortgage on the house was also something you're keen to make sure is paid out if something happens to you and that was $625,000. So, we've added the $300,000 in school fees, the $500,000 in living expenses and the $625,000 in debt to come to an insurance cover amount of $1,425,000. And we've agreed I'll give you terms and conditions on a policy at that amount and at $1,500,000. Does that sound like everything we've discussed and everything you want to cover Bill?"*

This pause enables the prospective customer to reflect on why they've chosen to engage with you in the insurance conversation. It causes them to acknowledge the problems you've helped them uncover and it highlights the value that could be achieved, if they put the right cover in place. It also gives you a great platform to explain where you're taking them from, and where the solution you're about to propose will take them to.

Signal the
Importance and Expectation
of a Decision

When you present a solution, the more focused you are on getting to the close, the more likely it is you'll engage in behaviour that causes objections.

There's a natural tension when you present a solution. You're a little tense on whether they'll say "yes" and the person you're presenting to is a little tense around potentially having to make a decision. You can reduce this tension by signalling the importance and expectation of making a decision.

What we want to do is create a shared set of expectations around the importance of deciding whether they want to take the cover, or accept the risk without cover. Some of you might think this is a little aggressive – and you can soften it, but here's an example of how I would suggest you prime the person's mind for making a conscious decision and accepting that "thinking about it" is a decision to remain uncovered.

SALESPERSON *"...Does that sound like everything we've discussed and everything you want to cover Bill?"*

BILL "Spot on."

SALESPERSON *"Great. I'll provide the solution that enables you to cover all of that. Before we get into the detailed part of the solution, there are two things that are important for you to understand. The first is that the pricing I provide is based on the all-clear on your medical health. If the health questions and any checks show something that could cause health issues, that can result in certain health* *problems being excluded or a higher premium. Does that make sense, Bill?"*

BILL "Yeah. I'm pretty confident all that will be fine."

SALESPERSON *"Great to hear, Bill and I'm hoping for the same. The second thing that's important is for you to understand is that right now you're not covered for all the things we discussed. No cover is in place until you give me the go ahead. So, once I've presented the solution, I'll need to formally ask you for that go ahead. Does that make sense, Bill?"*

BILL "Yeah, sure."

Create
Agreement Early

Research is telling us that when people agree on something early in a solution presentation, two very important things happen. The first is that rapport increases. The second positive outcome, which flows from the first, is that the lift in rapport makes the person more agreeable and more likely to continue to agree.

Similar research also tells us that where disagreement occurs early in the solution presentation, the opposite happens.

What this means for you is that you need to be deliberate about creating agreement early in the presentation. You also need to be deliberate about avoiding anything contentious that could cause disagreement.

This is another reason you need to do a great job of confirming everything they've told you that has been considered in creating the solution. Because you're just repeating back what they've told you, the probability of agreement is high. If there's strong disagreement, you haven't been listening, and you'll get what you deserve!

Confirm Your Professionalism
and Expertise

People are more likely to agree with and follow the guidance (and advice) provided by someone they perceive to be an expert.

We've discussed the importance of building your credibility in Chapter 9, so I'm not going to go over all of that again. Reconfirming their situation and what's driving their needs establishes greater credibility in the solution you're offering.

Doing this in a structured and clear manner shows that you've listened, and that builds your credibility. Being precise in your numbers and avoiding the tendency to just round them up builds your credibility. Taking your time and not being in a rush creates the perception that you're confident and not desperate for a deal. That also builds your credibility. Setting an expectation on the need to decide reminds them that you're serious about helping them cover the risk they've told you about. That also builds your credibility. And all of this can be done without having to provide any advice.

I hope this is giving you a sense that everything you've been doing up to this point is all coming together to make your solution presentation significantly more likely to translate into business for you and the right cover for the person you're engaging.

Customer centricity has major rewards for those willing to do the work.

Ethically Leverage
Their Urgency

I'm not a massive fan of leveraging urgency strategies to close deals.

Urgency, which is a form of scarcity, causes people to make rash decisions and while you might think it creates a great opportunity to "close someone", people generally come back to their senses and feel cheated or remorseful about buying. I'm not suggesting you should never leverage urgency or scarcity, I'm just reminding you to always put ethics first.

Don't get into the mindset that just because something is compliant that it's ethical. To test whether something is ethical, I would prefer you to be asking questions like,

"Would I be happy if someone were doing this to my Mum?"

rather than,

"Will I get in trouble with compliance for doing this?"

Enough said on that.

Situations where I believe it is appropriate and ethical to leverage a sense of urgency include strategies like the following.

SALESPERSON *"Before I go through the solution Bill, it's worth mentioning that from an insurance perspective you still sit in the band we consider relatively young. There's a lot of benefit in getting insurance at your age because your pricing should be lower because of that. Let's go through the solution."*

OR

"Bill, something I want you to consider as we go through the solution is that right now you have a clean bill of health. If we confirm that through the health questions I'll need to ask, that will mean you can get access to insurance with no health exclusions. It really is the best time to put something in place, because once you've suffered a medical condition, you don't get a second chance to place cover with no exclusions in place. Does that make sense?"

OR

"Bill. One more thing before we go through the solution: you mentioned you were heading off on holiday next week. I'm keen to get the cover in place before you take off. So, if you have any questions or concerns, please make sure you bring them up as I go through the solution with you. Is that OK?"

As you can see from the above, there will be situations where the customer's personal situation creates credible urgency for deciding and getting the cover in place. Commit to using this ethically, and you'll promote better decisions.

Celebrate Eligibility

Health questionnaires and getting health checks is a daunting process. I can remember when I took out my first major policy, being incredibly concerned about the probability I had skin cancers. I grew up in the sun, and in the seventies and eighties, we were sun-conscious, but not really too smart about it. I remember my little sister and I having an argument about whether it was "sunbathing" or "sun baking"!

It's easy to get a little blasé about the health questions, but when people get through their medicals and are accepted for insurance, they generally experience a significant sense of relief. That's a great opportunity for you to celebrate it and ethically leverage eligibility as a reason to keep moving forward to a decision. That would go something like the following.

SALESPERSON *"Great news, Bill. You are as healthy as you said you were, and you've been accepted. Other than the suicide exclusion we talked about, there's not a single exclusion. So you get to put an exclusion-free policy in place and from here on in, you'll be covered. Now the only other thing we need to discuss is…"*

I can appreciate that it might not seem that exciting to you, but I should also point out that this is a habit I've observed in nearly every successful phone insurance salesperson.

Trial Close Throughout the Presentation

Another habit I've observed to be consistently associated with success is effective trial closing throughout the solution presentation. What you want to avoid is going through the entire solution and then finding out that the person wasn't happy about something or had objections that weren't mentioned when you covered a certain area of the solution. Simple prompts like,

"Are you happy with that, Bill?"

or

"Does that sound good to you, Bill?"

as you complete each part of the solution presentation tend to reduce any objections at the end.

REMEMBER –
IT'S ALL ABOUT THEM

There's probably nothing incredibly new for many of you in this chapter, but I hope that by reminding you of all these important strategies you'll be inspired to get someone in your team or business to do some observations of your solution presentations and give you some feedback. Remember, knowing is not doing and just because none of these strategies may be new to you, it doesn't necessarily mean that you're executing all of them to a level of excellence when you present your solutions.

Something to keep in mind is that for the person you're helping, this is a big deal. It's often the first time they've purchased insurance, and it's a big step in their financial life. Don't take that for granted. Avoid just going through the motions, no matter how experienced you are. The more you treat it like it's the first time you've sold insurance, and the more they sense your commitment and interest, the better the customer experience is going to be. The solution presentation is an important moment for both you and the prospective customer. Treat it with that respect, and the more likely it is that all that hard work you did will result in success for you and the new customer.

CHAPTER THIRTEEN

ASKING FOR DECISIONS

DO WE NEED TO SPEAK ABOUT CLOSING?

I was tempted to leave this chapter out.

Not because "closing the sale" isn't important. As a salesperson, you can't achieve ROI, for you or your company, if you're not turning your hard work into new customers. I considered not writing about closing because one of the outcomes of a truly customer-centric sales process is that the prospective customer closes themselves. They literally get to the end of (or part way through) your solution presentation and confirm they're ready to put the solution into place.

Having said that, part of the reason they close themselves is you've been following the path I've set out for you in all the previous steps. You've been closing decisions and building a sense of commitment throughout the conversation. It's worth revisiting this and considering how commitment and the desire to act consistently impact the final decision to move ahead with the insurance solution you've offered.

I want to make sure you absolutely understand how the Principle of Commitment relates to successful conversion and closing. To do that, let's have a discussion about Apple People.

WHY DO PEOPLE BECOME APPLE FANATICS?

Our office in Sydney is just down the road from the Apple Store on the corner of George and King Streets. The Apple store is truly a temple of technology. Everything about the store tells you amazing products are what you'll find inside those doors. Apple has done a brilliant marketing job of creating a choice people need to make about their identity.

You're either an "Apple Person", or you're something else. It's not even Apple or Microsoft anymore. If you're an Apple Person, you own an iPhone despite there being many phones on the market that are just as functional and lower cost. You'll be more likely to own an Apple computer despite there being many other, just as functional and lower cost, computers on the market. You probably access your internet television through an AppleTV box despite the fact there are many other cheaper boxes available that are just as functional. You'll probably also be an iTunes or Apple Music user.

If you are an Apple Person, I want you to notice the reaction you had, when I suggested above that there are alternative products that are just as good.

I have little doubt you rapidly came up with a multitude of reasons why I was wrong. These justifications and beliefs about Apple made it very clear to you that your purchasing decisions were the right ones. Some of you are probably in the "defend Apple to the death" club. Ask yourself this – are there any other brands or products you own that you are this passionate about defending?

The big difference between owning an Apple product and owning other products, is that the purchase of an Apple product literally creates an identity. When a person takes on the identity of "Apple Person", they become significantly more likely to behave in a way that is consistent with that identity. That includes telling everyone else how good Apple products are, not complaining about the high price of Apple products and purchasing other products from the Apple range.

If you are an Apple Person, have a look around the house and tell me how many Apple products you own. (Including all the old ones you retired.) If you're not an Apple Person, I'm sure you know what I'm talking about. I live with one. And when she goes shopping at Apple, they don't need to close her. They just need to help her buy the Apple solution that best meets her needs and then get out of her way, so she can pay for it!

Why are we talking about Apple People? Because knowing that there are Apple People out there reminds us our insurance conversations should build a person's Loving Protector and Provider identity.

THE LOVING PROTECTOR AND PROVIDER IDENTITY

I've been going on about Apple People because I want you to understand that the more someone takes on an identity that is consistent with purchasing a product, the more likely it becomes that they will buy.

When a couple becomes pregnant and takes on the identity of parents, they go crazy buying baby stuff. When a person buys their first home, they take on the identity of homeowner, and start buying all sorts of homewares. And when a person takes on the identity of someone who needs to protect and provide for their loved ones, they buy insurance. I call this identity the "Loving Protector and Provider" identity.

The insurance conversation we've been discussing throughout this book is all about creating that identity for the person you're speaking to. The more you help someone build a "Loving Protector and Provider" identity throughout the conversation, the more likely it is they'll do the right thing and put the right cover in place. The stronger that identity, the more likely it is that they'll be prepared to spend a little more on premiums to make sure the right cover is in place. The stronger that identity, the less likely it is that they'll avoid making the decision and leaving those they love unprotected. Importantly, the more you help them engage with this identity, the more likely it is that the insurance will survive tight budget moments and the temptation to cancel in the future.

IDENTITY
(AND CLOSING) IS ALL
ABOUT COMMITMENT

We've been on a journey throughout this book, and I've been asking you to commit to the customer-centric way.

I've asked you to commit to being a salesperson who's more focused on helping people buy the right cover than you making a sale. I've challenged you to commit to achieving a level of excellence in your sales skills and a customer focus that drives both compliant and customer-centric engagement. I've challenged you on this throughout this book, because I know the only way you will sustainably make the changes I'm asking you to, is if you adopt a more customer centric identity.

The more you think of yourself as a customer centric salesperson, the more you'll habitually sell that way.

For some of you, this will mean some small changes to the way you engage customers and a more deliberate approach to using strategies that you know work. For many of you, it will require more significant changes and require you to unlearn habits and beliefs, that have been shared by peers and possibly coached into you by leaders and other trainers. Either way, I promise you that the rewards are significant for both you and the customer if you are willing to adopt a customer centric identity.

Let's go through what you get out of selling the protect and provide way.

In Chapter 4, we explored how to create problem acknowledgement and bring the customers' real needs to the surface. If you do this well, you'll be speaking to a person who has made a voluntary, specific and open commitment to having a problem that needs to be resolved. How much would you pay me per lead, if I could promise you people, in that mental and emotional state?

In Chapter 5, we explored how to build Value Expectations. I've given you strategies for gaining commitments to affordability, consistency with goals and values, value beyond price and a commitment to you and the value you bring to the person's insurance purchasing journey. How much would you pay me per lead, if I could guarantee you people, that were in that mental and emotional state? In Chapter 9, we explored how to gain mutual trust through a combination of rapport and credibility building. When two parties have mutual trust, decision making is easier, and closing is a formality. Imagine how much easier your role would be if you consistently created this dynamic between you and those considering their insurance options.

In Chapter 10, I gave you specific strategies for building key commitments through the effective use of questions. We know that when people share information and make statements they become more committed to behaving consistently with those statements. You now have a clearly defined strategy for moving away from talking and telling and towards asking and commitment building.

In Chapter 11, we explored the magic of gaining permission before offering solutions. We learned this builds even higher levels of commitment. I shared the IDEA Model to give you a valuable checklist of commitments you should strive to achieve before you offer a solution. Commitments that are all consistent with acting to do the right thing and protect and provide for loved ones.

And in Chapter 12, we explored how to present your solutions in a manner that connects them to all the commitments that have been made by the prospective customer throughout the insurance purchasing journey. If you've done the work throughout the insurance purchasing journey to gain these commitments, people literally can't say "no" to putting the right cover, or the cover they can afford, into place. They will have taken on the Loving Protector and Provider identity.

And as a bonus, selling in a customer-centric manner almost definitely guarantees that you'll differentiate yourself from others who are just focused on selling them insurance and competing on price over needs.

I can't guarantee you'll win every opportunity, but all this commitment to the customer's interests radically increases the probability a decision will be made and that you will be rewarded for the hard work you've done.

SOME CLOSING WISDOM

I will share a few specific scripts and strategies you might consider using at the close of your solution presentation. But before I do, I want to share some valuable closing wisdom that I've picked up over the past 20 years:

The Harder the Close –
The Bigger the Remorse

I cringe when people tell me about the big close they executed to turn the unwinnable opportunity into a deal. The story is generally told in a way that makes it sound like they wrestled a 20-foot crocodile into submission. The salesperson is always the hero of the story. The problem with this in the customer-centric sales process is the person buying insurance is the one that's meant to leave the purchase feeling like the hero. That's what keeps them committed to the purchase. It's what causes them to tell their friends that they need to speak to their insurance professional. It's also what keeps them committed to the value they achieve each month when they pay their premiums.

Every action has an equal and opposite reaction. Close hard and you should expect significant buyer remorse, which leads to cancellations and a person who's more likely to remain uncovered or underinsured. If you're using the hard close as your core sales weapon, you're more likely to be a villain than a hero!

Avoid the Big Mistake

Whether you're able to offer advice or not, by the time you've presented the solution all the required thinking and information sharing should have been done. There literally shouldn't be a need for a customer to think about the solution, because it has been built entirely based on their needs and numbers. But so often, insurance salespeople get to the end of a customer-centric solution presentation and ask,

"So, what do you think?"

There is a massive problem with this.

It takes the customer out of a solution0focused and committed mindset and back into a problem-solving mindset. When a customer is in a problem-solving mindset, they are much more likely to procrastinate and put off a decision. I think you know how I feel about people leaving the conversation, heading back out into the risky world we live in, and being in a state of "thinking about" putting the right cover in place.

Nobody plans for a heart attack, car crash or other insurance event. It just happens. And if it does, the fact someone was thinking about their insurance is going to be very little comfort to the loved ones left behind with inadequate or nonexistent cover.

Know Your Close

To avoid the big mistake, you need to know what your close is going to be. Remember, the close is not a trick to get someone to buy. A customer-centric close is a strategy focused on helping people to decide. Your goal is to help them make a conscious decision, then and there, on whether they want to provide adequate cover for those they love or leave the conversation without putting that cover in place.

All prospective customers and all insurance conversations are not the same. This means that the same closing strategy will not necessarily provide you with the same result in each insurance conversation in which you engage. You need to plan for the close when you plan for your solution presentation. And you need to have options, to make sure you can react or respond, to what might happen throughout that part of the conversation.

Having said this, planning for the close is more important than having options, so at the very least make sure you know your close and plan for when you'll use it. This is the only way you'll avoid the big mistake.

More Closing Options
Creates Higher Conversion

The best strategy will depend very much on the customer's situation, the level of commitment they've provided and the medium through which you're presenting. By medium, I mean over the phone, video conference or face to face. If you're presenting solutions via email, you shouldn't expect an optimal conversion rate. Let me share several closing options you might consider using:

The Direct Close – The more concerned and anxious you are about asking for a person's business, the more anxious and concerned they will be about deciding. Often a direct request for the business is the best way to reduce your anxiety and increase the prospective customer's confidence.

SALESPERSON *"That's great, Bill. And you're right about the extra amount covering living expenses. Can I put that in place for you now?"*

The Reverse Close – The reverse close is a close that many salespeople prefer, because it feels a little safer and less direct. This closing strategy causes the prospective customer to either confirm you should move forward or provide any concerns/objections they may have to moving forward.

SALESPERSON *"That's great, Bill. And you're right about the extra amount covering living expenses. Is there anything else we need to discuss, before we put all of that cover in place for you?"*

The Optional Close – This is an effective strategy because it meets the prospective customer's need for choice and it provides them with options, that all result in cover being put in place.

SALESPERSON *"That's great, Bill – and you're right about the extra amount covering living expenses. Would you like to include those extra living expenses, or would you prefer me to put the lower amount of cover in place for you today?"*

The Decision Close – In Chapter 13, we discussed signalling the importance and expectation of deciding. If you've leveraged that strategy when you offered your solution, you can remind the customer of this as part of your close. You might use this when you know the person really needs to put cover in place but is sitting on the fence.

SALESPERSON *"That's great, Bill – and you're right about the extra amount covering living expenses. As I've mentioned before Bill, I can't make a recommendation on whether you should or shouldn't take the extra cover to do that. But I can ask you to decide on whether we leave this discussion with the cover in place or not. I need to remind you that nobody's family has ever been able to make an insurance claim because their mother or father was thinking about buying insurance. (Pause) Can we set you up with that cover now Bill?"*

This certainly isn't an exhaustive list of all the closes you could use, but these are sufficient closing strategies for you to use in most selling situations you'll encounter. Focus on mastering these four strategies to a level of excellence, and then consider adding others to your sales tool kit.

The Pressure of Silence

I am a fan of Brian Tracy for all he's contributed to the profession of sales over the past 40 years. I've read so many of his books over the years I need to apologise for not being able to find which one this quote came from. One wonderful piece of wisdom I picked up from his vast number of books was this,

"The only credible pressure you can ever use in a selling situation is the pressure of silence."

So often, salespeople nullify the power of an effective closing strategy because they can't shut up after they've used it. I use that harsh language deliberately because people who can't shut up generally need strong language to make them pay attention! Let me give you a classic example of this:

SALESPERSON *"That's great, Bill – and you're right about the extra amount covering living expenses. Would you like to include those extra living expenses or would you prefer me to put the lower amount of cover in place for you today?" (Pause)*

Great closing question. The customer is processing and about to speak, and the salesperson can't handle the silence and must speak. This is what comes out of their mouth:

SALESPERSON *"...Would you like to include those extra living expenses or would you prefer me to put the lower amount of cover in place for you today?" (Pause) "We can always put more cover in place for you later if you change your mind."*

The customer was just about to either say yes or share a minor concern with the salesperson. But they filled the silence with another question – a question that implies they may be making the wrong decision today and that they can fix that mistake in the future. In one moment of madness, the salesperson has derailed the customer's decision-making process and made the customer think about putting cover in place "later". It doesn't take a rocket scientist to realise that this has significantly reduced the probability of a decision and the right cover being put in place.

MAKE THE DECISION
THE PRIORITY

I want to remind you of two things that are very important when it comes to the ethics of closing.

The first is that if the customer has a clear need for cover, you should have no fear of challenging them to decide on whether they will leave the conversation covered, or "thinking about it" (which includes shopping around). When your intention is to create clarity on the risk of failing to make a decision, you're being customer centric and should feel and act in a courageous manner. If you behave this way and they fail to decide today, you make it more likely that they'll want to speak with you when they are ready to act.

The second is that you shouldn't try to close people who don't have a clear need for cover. You shouldn't get in their way or turn them away if they want to buy cover. It's not your place to tell people what they can and can't do, but you shouldn't be doing anything that promotes the purchase of cover that will not meet a clearly understood need. Focus on helping people make decisions and the sales will take care of themselves without the need for aggressive closing.

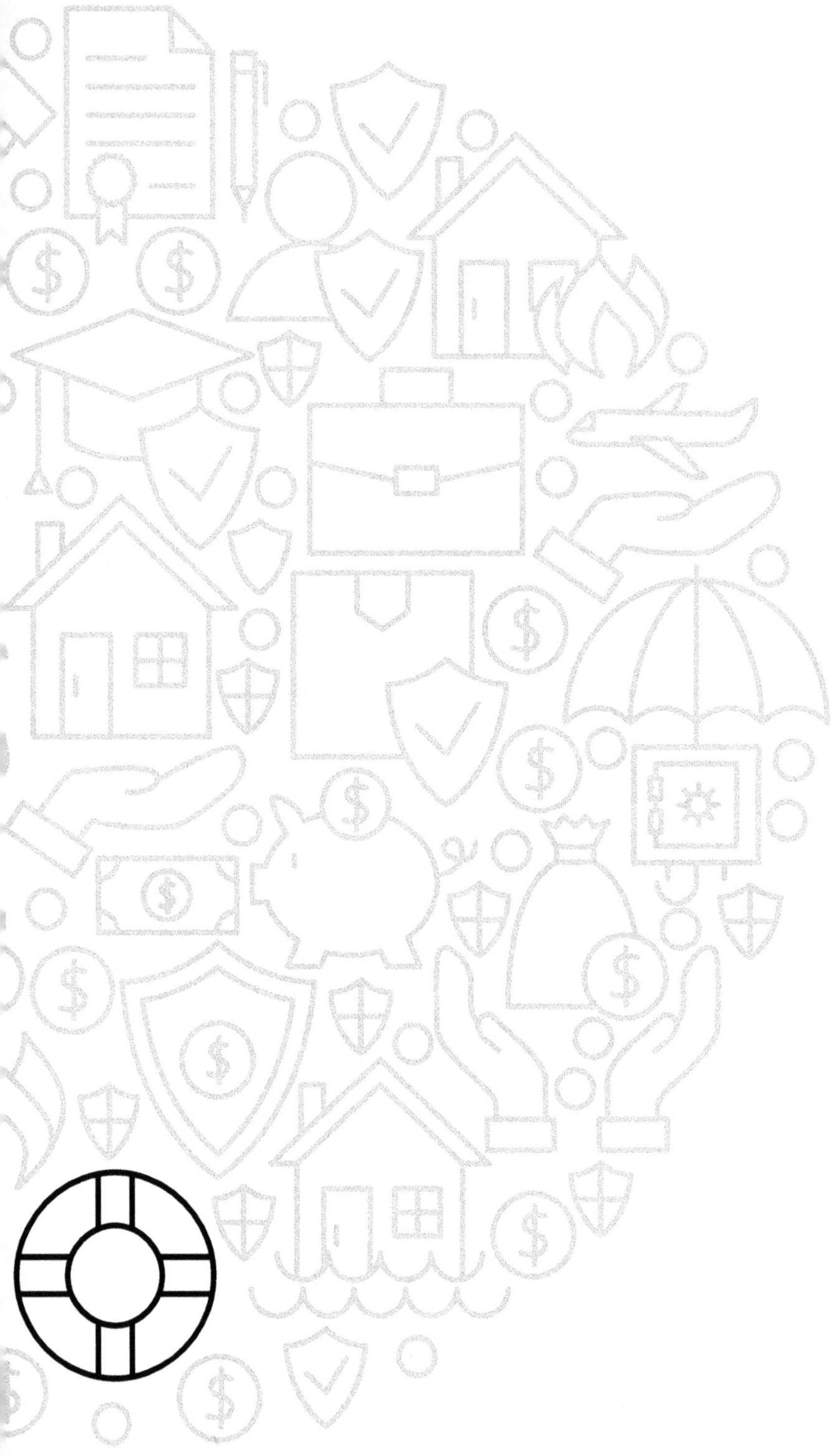

CHAPTER FOURTEEN

HANDLING OBJECTIONS

OBJECTIONS SIGNAL LAZINESS AND SELF-CENTRED SALES BEHAVIOUR

I imagine many of you read the title above and went,

"Thanks a lot, Dean. You're really making me feel great about myself. How do you know that all the objections I get are my fault?"

My apologies if you made yourself feel that way and had that internal dialogue with yourself. But the simple reality is that most objections a salesperson experiences reflect the way they are selling rather than what they're selling. If you had all the commitments we've discussed and you had gained permission effectively, you would not be experiencing objections at the end of the sales process. You would be prompting these earlier in the sales process and either helping the prospective customer move through them or opting out of the solution offering part of the insurance journey.

Remember, it doesn't make sense to try to sell to someone who is not ready to buy.

LET'S TALK
OBJECTIONS ANYWAY

Having said the above, I still need to acknowledge that insurance is probably the toughest product in the world to sell.

I know you'll face objections even when you're engaging people who know they have a need. This will happen because the desire to avoid contemplating and discussing death in detail is a strong one. I know that even the most credible of reasons for engaging in the discussion will often be met with objections. And I know that even if you're doing a great job, you'll face objections driven far more by fear than common sense or reason.

It's a tough game you've chosen to play, but that's why it's so rewarding both personally and financially. Despite the objections you'll need to face to help people buy the right cover, this profession is amazing if you choose the customer-centric way. That includes striving for excellence in your sales skills, behaviours and beliefs. Let's discuss the skills, behaviours and beliefs you need to develop in relation to the art of avoiding and handling objections.

AVOIDING
OBJECTIONS

If you've achieved a high level of Problem Acknowledgement and a high level of Value Expectation using the strategies we discussed in Chapters 4 and 5, you'll experience very few objections (if any) as you offer solutions and ask for outcomes (including decisions).

If you are facing common objections on a regular basis, make sure you commit to doing more than just defining and practising your response strategies. Take some time out to consider what you could be doing earlier in the insurance conversation to avoid these objections or, at the very least, drive a reduction in how often they arise.

ENGAGING PROSPECTIVE CUSTOMERS AND REDUCING COMMON OBJECTIONS

The excuses people use to avoid a conversation about their death and the impact this would have on their loved ones are common. It's difficult to avoid these objections, because we're yet to engage the prospective customer. But there are strategies we can employ to reduce and potentially avoid engaging a prospective customer in an objectional state of mind.

Make the Connection

People often react badly to someone engaging them where they experience "stranger danger". We explored that in Chapter 8 when we discussed the importance of creating a connection between yourself and the prospective customer as early as possible in the initial engagement. Remember, we can make connections using referrals, LinkedIn engagement, highlighting common connections, making product connections and a host of other strategies that reduce "stranger danger".

If you're experiencing a lot of objections when you reach out to prospective customers, you need to do the work on building better connections and executing this strategy in a confident and comfortable manner.

Sound Like a Peer on the Phone

The more comfortable and confident you sound when you engage a prospective customer, the more likely it becomes that they will respond positively. It never ceases to amaze me how many successful alpha-male insurance salespeople sound like a bumbling Hugh Grant from *Four Weddings and a Funeral* when they follow someone up after a networking event, or even off the back of a referral.

Sounding like a peer means that you need to "do the work" and know how you'll make the connection, how you'll explain the reason for the call and how you'll translate that into a meeting or an insurance conversation over the phone. Another aspect you should also consider is your physiology. The way you sit or stand will have a very significant impact on the way you feel and the tone of your voice.

Avoid a Binary Succeed or Fail Mentality

If you mentally set yourself up for failure, you're significantly more likely to perform in a way that increases the probability of failure. Which person do you think is likely to feel more comfortable and confident about making a call?

Insurance salesperson number one met someone at a networking event two days ago and is about to call them. If they are able to successfully set up a meeting, they consider the call a success. If they fail to get a meeting organised, they consider the call a failure.

They have a binary succeed/fail outcome mindset, which sets them up for a high probability of experiencing failure both mentally and emotionally.

Insurance salesperson number two met the same person at the same event. The next morning, they sent off a short email saying it was great to meet them, mentioned something that was discussed and let the prospective customer know they would call over the next few days. They considered all the outcomes that could be achieved in the call. They're keen to build their credibility and follow up as promised. They're keen to know whether the prospective customer met anyone else interesting at the networking event. They're keen to organise a meeting, but appreciate that it may take multiple engagements. They're keen to create a perception of value in an interesting article they plan to share following the call. They're keen to know more about the partnership the person is involved in. They're keen to get an understanding of whether the person has recently done a review and whether the partnership has considered life insurance as part of a buy/sell strategy. And they're keen to build their personal brand within the business community that attends the networking event.

The probability of achieving two to three of these outcomes in the call is high, even if no meeting is secured. By considering, planning for and seeking to achieve a broader range of outcomes, they make success more likely. This builds confidence before the call and makes them more likely to sound like a peer and come across as someone worth meeting. It builds confidence during the call because, as they achieve smaller outcomes, they feel better about the call.

And it creates higher levels of confidence after the call, even if the meeting is not achieved this time.

If you want to sound like you deserve a meeting, you need to set yourself up mentally to feel like you deserve a meeting.

Respond Positively
to "How Are You Going?"

I am sincere when I tell you that I have heard salespeople respond to this question with,

"Better than dead"

and

"I'm hanging in there"

Wow! Do you think that really made me want to meet with them? I'm not suggesting you need to say,

"I'm FANTASTIC!"

but you do need to think through how you'll respond to this common question and what sort of impression you want to create.

Listen!

I am sincere when I tell you I have heard the following exchange when reviewing insurance calls.

SALESPERSON *"How are you going?"*

> **BILL** "Pretty bad. I've just found out I'm being made redundant."

SALESPERSON. *"Oh. OK. Well anyway, I'm calling about an income protection product that links to the life insurance you recently purchased..."*

It never ceases to amaze me how many salespeople ask,

"How are you today?"

with no real intention of listening to the customer's verbal or emotional response. That creates significant disconnection and increases the likelihood of objections dramatically.

ENGAGING PROSPECTIVE CUSTOMERS AND RESPONDING TO COMMON OBJECTIONS

In an ideal world, our delivery would be outstanding, and people wouldn't be able to resist speaking to us. Unfortunately, I'm still working on the script that will give you 100% cut through with zero objections. I suggest that you forget about waiting for that and focus instead on making sure you've done the work to respond to common objections, to setting a meeting, or engaging in the insurance conversation over the phone.

We can plan for these objections because they generally fall into four categories: irrational aggression, no interest, already covered and too busy. Let's discuss these a little further:

Irrational Aggression

To sell insurance over the phone, you need thick skin, because the sheer number of people you'll be calling and nature of the leads mean that you're going to experience some irrational and aggressive responses. I won't use examples here because I would prefer not to write out the sort of language I commonly hear when this sort of objection is experienced.

My suggestion is don't try to get beyond this objection. You have better things to do than trying to help someone in this state of mind.

But you can't afford to let their bad state of mind impact your state of mind. There are three things you need to avoid when you experience this sort of behaviour. The first is to avoid personalising their bad behaviour. Personalising happens when you take responsibility for something that really isn't your fault. This is a very common behaviour in people that fail in the insurance profession. The language you use to respond to this type of objection is very important. If you apologise for upsetting the person, you are subconsciously personalising their bad behaviour. My suggestion is to let them finish what they're screaming at you, take a deep breath and say the following:

SALESPERSON *"I'm sorry you're upset by the call today, Bill. I'll leave you to your day, and I hope things improve for you. Thanks for taking the call." (Pause)*

Notice I haven't asked you to say,

"I'm sorry for upsetting you"

You didn't upset them. They upset themselves. The pause at the end enables them to hang up, make a statement that helps them feel justified for their poor behaviour so they can hang up, or apologise for being horrible. If you avoid personalising their bad behaviour, you can't really lose.

The other two things you need to make sure of when this happens are avoiding making their behaviour permanent or pervasive. This language comes from Martin Seligman's book *Learned Optimism,* which is a must-read for all insurance professionals including coaches, compliance professionals and senior leaders.[14]

"Permanent" refers to the length of time you believe the customer's bad mood and behaviour is likely to last. The more optimistic and successful salesperson says to themselves,

"Wow. He's having a bad day today. Maybe he'll be in a better mood next time I or someone else in the team calls him"

When you make another person's bad mood, lack of interest, indecision or other negative behaviour temporary, you're much more likely to maintain a positive state of mind and realise that today's "no" is often tomorrow's "maybe" or "yes".

"Pervasiveness" refers to how much a single encounter with a customer in a bad mood impacts the rest of your day, feelings about your role and feelings about other prospective customers you need to engage later that day. People who fail in insurance, generally globalise bad behaviour. Something like this happens and they tell themselves,

"Man, nobody wants to speak to us, and when we get through, people are always angry"

But the more optimistic and resilient insurance salesperson knows they just need to isolate and compartmentalise a single prospective customer's bad mood and behaviour. The ability to isolate by saying to yourself,

"Wow. He's having a bad day. I'm glad most of the people we speak to aren't like that when I call"

is a behaviour associated with higher levels of success in insurance sales. Where you can isolate poor behaviour to a single person, point in time or other specific aspect of the dynamic that has just occurred, you're much more likely to maintain momentum in your day and not let a negative exchange slow you down. Please don't underestimate the importance of what I've just shared. Take the time to read Seligman's book on how your mindset will dramatically impact your success or failure in the insurance industry.

No Interest

You really shouldn't be surprised when you engage a prospective customer and get this objection early in the conversation. It's a completely natural response and, once again, the place to start is not taking it personally. Generally, this is just a defence mechanism against "stranger danger". If you receive this objection, your strategy should be to test it. People will generally let this one go and give you a single opportunity to respond effectively. My suggested response is generally something along the following lines.

> **BILL** "I'm not interested in life insurance."

> **SALESPERSON** *"I can appreciate that, Bill. It's not the most comfortable topic. Do you have any cover outside of your super?"*

> **BILL** "No."

> **SALESPERSON** *"Understood, Bill. Have you ever considered whether the cover you have in super (group cover) would be enough to cover the things that matter to you?"*

> **BILL** "Not really."

> **SALESPERSON** *"That's pretty normal, Bill. How about I ask you a few questions to help you get an idea of how much cover would be ideal, and then you can check your super to see if you have enough. If you've got plenty of cover, that's great. But if that's not the case, then we can talk some more. Is it okay if I just ask you a few questions?"*

I'm not suggesting that this or other similar response strategies are going to work every time, but knowing what your strategy is going to be and practising it until you're able to confidently respond in these situations is most of the "battle".

I'm Already
Covered

As I've mentioned numerous times throughout this book, one of the things that concerns me most is the number of people that incorrectly believe they're covered. I choose to believe nobody would intentionally fail to provide and protect those they love. But so often this is what flows from this incorrect belief. When you hear this objection, imagine a family in mourning, surprised by the lack of cover in place. The person giving you this excuse won't get an opportunity to imagine this or think about it, because they'll be dead, or in a state that disables them from doing anything to protect and provide for those they love. I can appreciate that this sounds extreme, but this is the genuine consequence of accepting this objection and failing to at least test it.

My suggested response is generally something along the following lines:

BILL "I'm already covered, thanks."

SALESPERSON *"That's great, Bill. Is that just through your super or do you have standalone policies in place to make up for the shortfalls in your super?"*

BILL "What do you mean?"

SALESPERSON *"I've got cover through my super, too, Bill. Have you compared the cover you've got in the super to what you think you'll need if something does happen to you?"*

BILL "Not really."

SALESPERSON *"That's pretty normal, Bill. How about I ask you a few questions to help you get an idea of how much cover would be ideal and then you can check your super to see if you have enough. If you've got plenty of cover, that's great, but if that's not the case, then we can talk some more. Is it OK if I just ask you a few questions?"*

If all you achieve out of responding to this objection is opening their eyes to the potential gap in cover, you've done an important thing.

I'm Too Busy

I can appreciate that you may be tempted to respond with,

"Are you too busy to die?"

but I think we can do better than that, and we need to have empathy for people's responses.

They're not trying to be difficult. They've just had experiences that tell them most people engaging them are likely to waste their time. You're going to be the exception, but you need to get them past this excuse.

I imagine you want a response that takes them away from whatever else they're doing and causes them to give you their undivided attention. The customer-centric insurance professional is many things to many people, but one of them is not desperate. I suggest you leave them to their day and focus on handling this objection, in a manner that makes them feel more comfortable and open to your next engagement.

ALICE "I'm too busy right now."

SALESPERSON *"I understand completely, Alice. Is there a better time to call you back later today?"*

ALICE *"I'm too busy today?"*

SALESPERSON *"That's fine, Alice. I'm here 9am – 5 pm tomorrow and Friday. Which day would be best to call back?"*

You're probably being coached to try to nail down a specific time to call back and to use a more aggressive optional funnel strategy to achieve that. I can appreciate that this will work in many scenarios. My perspective is that creating a relationship and a softer approach is more appropriate at this early stage of the insurance conversation.

THAT'S A LOT OF DETAIL!

Given I started this chapter, suggesting that the customer-centric way should help you avoid objections altogether, I can appreciate that this involves quite a bit of detail.

I've provided scripted responses and thoughts on these common engagement objections, because a failure to conquer these is what causes so many great people to fail and leave the industry. A fear of engagement causes so many insurance professionals to slow down their new business development, and the concern I have with that is the most experienced people we have in our industry are not actively engaging more people in the insurance conversation.

I've provided you with the detail to make sure you can move past these common objections and spend more time with more people engaged in valuable insurance conversations.

THE DREADED
PRICE OBJECTION

Organisations that market on price and people who sell on price get the price-buying customer behaviour they deserve.

The fantastic thing about adopting a customer-centric approach and leveraging the PAVE approach is that it focuses the person you're engaging on the problem they need to solve and the value they should expect to gain if they say,

"Yes"

This will reduce their focus on the price they need to pay, and if you've done the work they'll have a clear understanding of the value above price they will achieve if they move forward.

When people object to the solution you've offered because the price of cover that meets their needs is too high, you shouldn't be concerned. They're not objecting to the cover in the solution you've helped them create. They do not deny the needs they've confirmed throughout the insurance conversation you've had. They're just telling you that they have a concern with paying that amount to protect and provide for the people they love. Or are they?

TESTING THE
PRICE OBJECTION

The most important skill you need to develop in relation to the price objection is the confidence and skill required to test it. Testing an objection is not about overcoming the objection. It's about getting a sense of whether the objection is a real concern or a negotiating strategy.

People are being told to negotiate with larger financial institutions. So, we shouldn't be surprised if the basis of the objection is purely a strategy aimed at getting a better price. Sometimes objections are also just an attempt to avoid the need to decide. Either way, testing the price objection is a better place to start than by responding to it. Testing an objection can be as simple as remaining silent after the objection or paraphrasing what they've just said. Paraphrasing goes something like this:

> **BILL** "$116 a month is pretty expensive."

> **SALESPERSON** *"Expensive?" (Asked as a question and followed by silence)*

> **BILL** "Yeah. Well, I was hoping to only pay about $80 a month."

> **SALESPERSON** *"OK?" (Silence)*

> **BILL** "But I hadn't really thought about living expenses and everything else."

> **SALESPERSON** *"I can appreciate that, Bill. Are the living expenses still something you're committed to covering with the insurance?" (Silence)*

> **BILL** "I guess so. I don't really want Mary to have to go back to work straight away."

> **SALESPERSON** *"OK, Bill. So, shall we go ahead with the cover that includes those?*

You will be amazed at how effective testing can be in removing what seems to be a significant pricing objection. What I like about this strategy is that it enables the prospective customer to figure things out for themselves. All you're doing is prompting them to consider whether their objection is about what they want to pay, or genuine affordability issues.

WHILE WE'RE ON AFFORDABILITY...

As I mentioned earlier, if you're selling on price, you deserve to get price objections.

Whether you can offer advice or not, you should be actively encouraging people to first consider their needs. Once those needs are clear, you should be providing them with terms and conditions (including premium pricing) on the insurance solution that meets those needs. Only when you've established that the right cover is beyond their financial means should you revert to cover levels determined by affordability.

I've listened to too many calls that sound like this:

> **BILL** "$116 a month is pretty expensive."

> **SALESPERSON** *"How about we take it down to $100 a month?"* *(Silence)*

> **BILL** "I'm not really sure."

> **SALESPERSON** *"OK. Let's make it $75 a month, and I'll tell you what cover you get for that. OK. So, $75 a month is going to get you $358,000 of cover. Are you happy with $75 a month?" (Silence)*

> **BILL** "I guess so. That definitely sounds more affordable."

This is not the customer-centric way, and I challenge whether it's ethical, despite arguably being compliant.

You may disagree with me, but if you do are you genuinely putting the customer's needs ahead of your need to sell something? Don't think that just because it's compliant and it results in sales, that a strategy is ethical or customer centric.

I can appreciate that this stance might not make me the most popular kid on the insurance block. I can also appreciate that many of your prospective customers may be engaging you purely based on "Give me a price".

But you and I know what makes for genuine customer centricity.

We've been on the journey together throughout this book. In your heart you know that simply quoting prices and finding a premium level at which someone will buy a policy is unlikely to ensure that the people they leave behind are protected or provided for. There's always the justification that "some insurance is better than none". But I wonder if that's what the agent who took care of my father's insurance told themself when they sold him his policy?

I'm calling out this common affordability approach as not being in the interest of the customer – and I can confidently tell you it's not in the interest of the families they leave behind. In my experience, it's happening because salespeople don't have the skills to sell outside of price. They don't have the confidence to respond to price-buying behaviour with empathy and a commitment to customer education on real needs beyond affordability.

The government needs to take some of the responsibility for this. Legislation around advice and affordability has created so many unintended consequences that are against the interests of families relying on the right amount of cover being put in place. Compliance teams supporting a focus purely on affordability have a lot to answer for and need to be challenged on this – and the organisations they're working for need to commit to doing the work to meet all aspects of the protect and provide test.

But that's all out of your control. As a professional insurance sales-person, you need to take responsibility for being the best you can be in the environment you're in.

RESPONDING TO THE PRICE OBJECTION

The more confident and skilled you are when a customer offers a price objection, the more likely you are to feel confident selling in a customer-centric manner. So, before we move on to the next chapter, let me offer you three levels of objection response strategy for price objections. These are in the order I hope you commit to mastering. It shouldn't surprise you that if you master the first two, you shouldn't have to revert to the last one too often.

BILL "I can't afford $116 per month."

SALESPERSON *"Sure, Bill. I can appreciate that this is an extra cost, but please consider that against leaving the family behind with the debt on the home of $400,000 and no living expenses to allow your partner to get things in order. Would you be comfortable with a lower cost option that didn't pay out all the debt?" (Silence)*

OR

"Sure, Bill. That's for $500,000 of cover. We can go one of two ways – you can tell me the minimum amount of cover you think would be enough for the family, and I can let you know what the premium will come down to (Pause) or you can give me an amount you think you could afford monthly and

I can let you know what cover that will give you. (Pause) Which would you prefer?" (Silence)

OR *(If you must)*

"Sure, Bill. What do you think you can afford to pay each fortnight?"

Once again, I want to make sure I'm clear. I understand there will be times when you need to roll back from the ideal solution that meets all the customer's needs to a lower cost option. That can absolutely be customer centric, but starting with affordability is not customer centric.

Affordability is one of a customer's needs, but it completely ignores the needs of the people that will be left behind if an insurance event occurs.

IT'S NOT ALL ABOUT OBJECTION HANDLING AND CLOSING

So often I'm engaged by senior people within large financial institutions and told up-front that what they need is a program around objection handling and closing. They have a firm belief that this is the path to higher levels of conversion.

I respond the same way every time. I let them know I can put together a program that meets those requirements and mobilise my team of experts to train it or help their people train those skills into the organisation. I know enough about influence to start with agreement and what I can do.

But then I move to the important question, which is,

"Why do you think your people are getting so many objections and finding it so hard to close?"

You've been on the journey with me throughout this book, and you know the answer to this question. If you're willing to commit to customer centricity, doing the work and helping people buy, I can promise you a lot more sales with a lot fewer objections and, consequently, little need to close.

Part of doing the work is being willing to invest your time and energy, so let's go to the last skill set in the ROI Sales Methodology.

CHAPTER FIFTEEN

NEXT STEPS

SUSTAINABLE
SUCCESS REQUIRES
AN INVESTMENT
OF TIME

How willing are you to invest in a relationship?

When I say "relationship", I'm not talking about a sale. I'm talking about a genuine relationship built on a deep understanding, mutual trust, doing the work to help the prospective customer buy the right cover and creating a sense of commitment that lives beyond the transaction involved in putting a policy in place.

My experience tells me that salespeople willing to invest in that type of relationship with every one they sell to experience all that being a sales professional should be. They enjoy the conversations in which they engage their prospective and existing customers. They effortlessly help people buy the right amount of cover. Where affordability is a challenge, they successfully sell what can be purchased. They receive referrals; they have passionate affiliate relationships with their customers who go out of their way to talk about and recommend them; they leverage testimonials and customers as part of their sales process and find it easier to turn a prospect into a willing partner on the insurance purchasing journey. Third parties like accountants and lawyers refer them because their clients speak so highly of the service and value they received when buying their insurance. They sleep well at night knowing they're ethical and, while compliance is important to them, their customer-centric behaviour means it's not an issue – and they prosper financially, not just when they sell the policy, but each year they review it and ensure the right protection is in place to adequately provide for the customer's loved ones in the event of an insurance claim being made.

If you want all of this, you need to be happy to invest more than a few meetings or a single call. The less time and effort you put into selling a policy, the less likely you'll reap the longer-term benefits of being truly customer centric and helping someone buy.

BUT IT'S DIFFERENT OVER THE PHONE

Why?

Seriously. Why should it be any different over the phone? Maybe you think that because you don't get to see the prospective customer face to face? Maybe you think that because sometimes you do sell a policy in a single phone call and that seems to be more time efficient? Maybe you think that because the level of advice you're allowed to offer is limited?

MORE EXCHANGE CREATES GREATER LOYALTY AND CUSTOMER CONFIDENCE

In my experience, the most successful phone insurance salespeople behave in very similar ways to the most successful face-to-face advisors. In most call centres I've consulted to, there's a very strong correlation between multi-call sales and two things.

By multi-call sale, I mean an insurance sale that requires multiple calls and isn't secured with a single "wham bam" call.

The first correlation is that the most consistently successful insurance salespeople (over the longer term) tend to make more multi-call sales. There are individual months where the Wham Bam Superstars top the leaderboard, but over a 12-month period the salespeople who are happy to invest tend to win out.

The second and arguably more important correlation is that the multi-call sales are significantly less likely to be cancelled in the 12 months following the sale. You know why I'm upset by this, but it also impacts the bottom line – so you and your organisation should be concerned about it too.

We know that the more exchange there is, the more rapport and liking there is, so this intuitively makes sense.

Despite this, so much effort is put into strategies to secure the policy in a single meeting or phone call. Where efforts needs to be invested, and strategy needs to be developed, is in order to upskill salespeople in maintaining a connection with a prospective customer that builds a stronger and more genuine relationship. Even in situations where the insurance cover is sold in a single call, organisations need to be encouraging and enabling their salespeople to reconnect and deliver customer experiences that build commitment to long-term relationships and confidence in the cover that's been purchased.

NEXT STEP
STRATEGY

I've studied what the best insurance salespeople do to ensure connection is maintained through a multi-call or multi-meeting sales process. There's a common set of strategies I've noticed nearly all great insurance professionals use to create higher levels of confidence and commitment to the ongoing sales process. Whether you sell insurance face to face or over the phone, this is a critical skill.

The following are the key aspects of next step strategies I've noticed used by the most effective insurance salespeople when the person they're speaking to asks for time to consider the terms and conditions, or to speak to a partner.

They Acknowledge and Agree
that it Makes Sense to Take Time
Out or Engage a Partner

Some of the better insurance professionals I've observed recommend this proactively.

The more comfortable and confident the prospective customer perceives you to be, the more comfortable they will be in maintaining a connection to you and making commitments around next steps. You don't want the person you're engaging to feel or think you're challenging them on their need to take time out or engage a partner. This sounds something like the following.

SALESPERSON *"Thanks for letting me know you need to do that, Jason. This is important because if you or your family need to make a claim, you don't get a second chance to make sure you put the right cover in place. How long do you think you'll need to think it over?"*

OR

SALESPERSON *"Thanks for letting me know you need to do that, Jason. This is important because if you or your family need to make a claim, you don't get a second chance to make sure you put the right cover in place. Are you likely to discuss that with James tonight?"*

They Confirm What Has
Been Achieved

The more effort someone puts into something and the more they feel that effort has achieved something, the more likely it is that they'll complete the task. So, before you let someone go away to think about things or engage a partner, you should remind them of what's been achieved. That sounds something like this:

SALESPERSON *"Jason. I just need to make sure that we're both on the same page with where the conversation and your cover is at. We've clarified the amount of cover you think you need and exactly what that will cover should something happen to you or James. We've taken you through the detailed health questions and confirmed that you qualify for exclusion-free cover other than the suicide exclusion for 13 months. So, that part of it is all done for you, and the result is great. Your premium for the $300,000 of cover will be $127 per month. I've confirmed that based on the information you've given me. James's cover would cost $113 per month, but that* *is subject to him going through the same detailed health questions as you've been through today and no conditions being identified that will impact his eligibility. Just to remind you, his premium is a little cheaper than yours, because of his occupation. I've also got your credit card details on file for monthly payments so that when you put the policy in place, there's no more administration to do on that front."*

Be thorough in explaining everything that has been achieved. This enables you to confirm that they have a clear understanding of what it is they need to think about and/or engage their partner around. It's good compliance practice, and it also builds commitment to coming back and finalising cover.

They Confirm that Cover is Not Yet in Place

You need to make sure that people don't leave the call or meeting under the mistaken impression that they're covered while they're thinking about it. This is something you often must make very clear, but you also need to avoid coming across as "hard selling" and deliberately creating fear.

It generally goes something like this:

SALESPERSON *"...I've also got your credit card details on file for monthly payments so that when you put the policy in place, there's no more administration to do on that front. So, we've covered a lot of ground today, but there's something I need to make sure you understand. (Pause) Between now and when you come back to me, there is no cover in place and you're not covered for any of the events we've discussed. (Serious and concerned tone – this should*

be genuine!) I just want to make sure you under-
stand that?" (Pause – silence)

They Offer Guaranteed
Acceptance Cover if Available

If you're in a country that doesn't use this terminology, I'll explain. Guaranteed acceptance is cover that excludes any pre-existing medical conditions and other common exclusions like suicide. It's often offered as a stop gap to cover a person between when they've confirmed they want cover but need to return more detailed medical information. It's also commonly offered when people want to cover a partner who is not available to go through the underwriting process.

In many phone sales scenarios, the person's payment details will be taken before they go through a detailed underwriting question-naire. This makes it relatively easy to put this sort of cover in place while they go away to think about things or engage a partner. In my experience, I've found the best phone insurance salespeople offer this as an option to ensure people are covered before they leave the current call. It goes something like this:

SALESPERSON *"Between now and when you come back to me, there is no cover in place, and you're not covered for any of the events we've discussed. (Serious and concerned tone – this should be genuine!) I just want to make sure you understand that?" (Pause – silence)*

JASON "Yeah." (Pause)

SALESPERSON *"Jason. I can't advise you on what to do, but would you like me to put your cover in place so you can take the time you need to think it through? It just means you're not rushed to make your decision. As*

I mentioned earlier, there's no obligation to continue. We refund the payment if you decide not to go ahead, and it's easy for me to process the first month's payment now and get your cover in place. Can I do that for you, Jason?"

They Reconfirm
Contact Details and a
Time to Reconnect

Whether the prospective customer chooses to cover themselves or not, the best in the business always reconfirm contact details as a priming mechanism to build greater commitment to the next conversation. Then they propose a high-level timeframe and ask for the other person to make it more specific. This builds commitment to following through on the promise to reconnect. That goes something like this:

SALESPERSON *"Thanks, Jason. You've got 30 days with no commitment to the policy, so that gives you plenty of time to speak to James, but I'm keen to get cover in place for James as well and take this off your "to do" list. So, can I just confirm that your email is* jason@ needscover.com *and that the best number for me to call you on will be the mobile which is 555 888 888? Are those details right, Jason?"*

JASON "Spot on." (Pause)

SALESPERSON *"Great, Jason. Now, if you're speaking to James tonight, will it work for you if I give you a call tomorrow?"*

JASON "Probably the day after would be better."

SALESPERSON *"Sure, Jason. Would this time of day suit you?"*

JASON "Yeah. That will work."

SALESPERSON *"OK. Great. So, I'll call you back at 2pm on the day after tomorrow, which is Thursday. Do you use an electronic diary on your phone, Jason?"*

JASON "Yes, I do."

SALESPERSON *"Brilliant. I'll send you an invite to that email address, so it's in your diary."*

JASON "Great."

They Clearly Articulate the Purpose and Desired Outcomes of the Next Call

As you'll understand by now, the clearer and more specific the commitment, the more likely a person is to behave consistently and follow through on what's agreed. So, it's smart to agree on the purpose of the next call and what the mutual expectations are on decisions and actions that will flow from the next meeting. That goes something like this:

SALESPERSON *"Thanks, Jason. And just to confirm, the goal for that call is to confirm you've spoken to James about the cover and everything we've been through in relation to covering debts and living expenses. If James and you are both comfortable we've got the right cover in place and it fits into the budget, we can confirm that your insurance cover will continue and I can get you out all the formal policy documentation. We can also tee up a time for me to speak to James and get his medical questionnaire completed and his insurance in place. Is there anything else or does that sound like it covers everything?"*

They Thank and Praise
the Prospective Customer

You know enough about the science of liking to understand why this is important, but there's more to it than that. The Law of Recency tells us that people are most likely to remember the last part of the call. This leaves a strong final impression that can be taken into the next call. It also re-energises the salesperson and gives them momentum for the next call. This obviously needs to be sincere, and the more you practice praise and gratitude as part of your normal communication, the more this will become part of the way you sell.

JASON "That's great, Dean. Very thorough."

SALESPERSON *"Thanks, Jason. I always appreciate feedback like that and at times worry that I'm a little too detailed, but it's important that we get this right. I really appreciate all the time you've spent considering what you need to cover to make sure both you and James are protected should anything happen to either of you. Have a great day, Jason, and speak to you Thursday."*

NEXT?

Wow. We've made it all the way through the nine steps and skill sets you need to develop to achieve mastery of the ROI Sales Methodology. I can appreciate that was a lot of work! It's probably become clear by now, that I'm not going to apologise for that.

Choosing the customer-centric way is about choosing to do the work. Salespeople, leaders, coaches and organisations that "do the work" get an amazing return on their investment.

CHAPTER SIXTEEN

ARE YOU COMMITTED TO PROTECTING AND PROVIDING?

Thanks for coming on the journey with me. If you've made it this far in the book, I know you're a person with the work ethic required to achieve excellence in your sales skills, behaviours and beliefs. I also know that it's likely to flow into the way you help people buy the right cover and ensure they protect and provide for the people they care for. I want to acknowledge you for both.

As you reflect on the ROI Sales Methodology, I want to leave you with a reminder that each step of the methodology is about earning the right to a sale, and an ongoing relationship with and support from the people to whom you sell.

Outcome Focus – This was all about you. But that's because only the strong can help the weak, and only the strong survive and thrive in insurance sales. It's an amazing profession and a terrible "job". Commit to being a customer-centric professional, focus your efforts daily, be deliberate about achieving a great return for your efforts, and you will be successful.

Credible Reasons – By choosing to develop your ability to engage with credible reasons, you've made the first step to truly engaging in a customer-centric manner. This alone takes you out of the "mediocrity bucket" of people who sell insurance as a "job" and in to the group of professionals in the industry. It also focuses you on the genuine needs of the prospective and existing customers you want to serve. This skill will enable you to earn an audience with more people and increase their receptiveness to engaging with you in the insurance purchasing journey.

Building Rapport and Credibility – You now understand trust is about more than just being likeable, and your commitment to building both credibility and rapport will enable you to rapidly earn trust in all the common selling situations you experience. It takes work to earn trust, but the payoffs and returns more than outweigh the effort required to be a likeable expert.

Explore and Listen – To be truly customer centric, your solutions and relationships must be supported by a deeper understanding of the prospective customer's needs and motivations. You've developed a deeper understanding of how to create needs through Problem Acknowledgement strategies. You've developed your ability to explore, and importantly, complemented that with a heightened understanding of how to listen and hear what's really been said. Your ability to explore and listen will position you to earn an understanding of the customer no matter what level of advice you're authorised to provide.

Gain Permission – You know your time is precious and that a quoting mentality is a sure-fire way to spend time with people who are not ready to buy. Your understanding of how to gain permission to offer solutions and build genuine commitment to making decisions will ensure that you earn the commitment required to turn great solutions into new customers.

Offer Solutions – The hard work you've done will make it easier to effectively match the customer's situation with the solution provided. You won't need to rely on a feature benefit dump to try to explain the value of your solution. Your work on creating a desire to solve acknowledged problems and taking advantage of expected value will flow through to your presentation and deliver a truly customer-centric experience.

Your solution presentations will enable you to earn a preference for doing business with you, from even the most challenging prospective customer.

Ask for Outcomes – Your understanding of the importance of decisions throughout the customer's insurance purchasing journey, along with the skills you've developed, will enable you to earn decisions at every stage of the journey in a manner that's consistent with helping the customer buy the right cover rather than you selling them insurance products.

Handle Objections – All of this will enable you to avoid most objections, but where concern and reluctance remain, you've developed the skills to understand and help prospective customers move beyond anything hindering the ability to put the right cover or the best affordable cover in place. Your skills in this area will enable you to earn actions that are consistent with protecting and providing the loved ones of any person you engage in the insurance conversation.

Next Steps – You're committed to a career as a professional and understand the importance of investing time and energy into relationships and the insurance purchasing journey of everyone you engage. This skill set will enable you to consistently earn momentum and ensure your hard work and commitment translates into sales for you and the right cover for those lucky enough to share their insurance purchasing journey with you.

This is the customer-centric way. This is what it takes to truly protect and provide.

BONUS CHAPTER

WHY GENERAL (BUSINESS) INSURANCE SALESPEOPLE MUST ENGAGE AROUND LIFE INSURANCE

This is an additional chapter for those of you who are more focused on selling general or business insurance. As a life insurance salesperson, there's a high probability that you rely on general insurance professionals in this space to send you referrals.

Either way, this chapter will help you engage business owners more effectively. If you need help in this area please touch base with my team around our Generating Life Leads program.

IS TALKING LIFE INSURANCE REALLY PART OF MY JOB?

If you truly care about the wellbeing of your business customers, the answer to this is "Yes." The more you understand the personal exposure most business customers have to economic hardship, the more you'll realise this is a must-have conversation.

PERSONAL INSURANCE AND THE BUSINESS OWNER

To build a business you need to be slightly crazy.

Even if you've managed to build a great business over the years, you will have endured cash flow crunches, over-reliance on key employees, the difficulty of moving customer relationships from the owners to the sales team, the challenge of maintaining a positive relationship with your business partner when things aren't going to plan and a whole raft of other challenges along the way. You've probably also paid yourself last for years, and worked for a wage that makes your hourly rate look like you were employed as a 15-year-old in McDonald's! (When I was when I was 15, five dollars an hour was a great deal)To endure these challenges, business owners need to be very good at remaining overly optimistic, even when the facts are telling them that they don't have a hope of surviving. You develop a tolerance for risk that is completely out of touch with reality and believe that no matter how big the problem is, you'll find a way to solve it and survive until you do.

I know, because I (and my business partner) have been through all of this as business owners.

It's taken nearly a decade to build a business that functions effectively without both of us present. I also know this because it's what most business owners talk about with the people they really trust. To the rest of the world (including our employees), we put on a brave face, but the reality is often very different to what others see, no matter how good the business looks on paper. What might surprise you is that the more growth a business owner is experiencing, the more likely they are to be facing major risks. The point I'm making here is that most businesses simply don't work if one of the owners dies or becomes unable to work in the business. And the problem with the optimism skills you develop to survive is that there's a high probability your personal life is significantly underinsured.

I know this because of what happened to my father's business when we lost him. What seemed to be an amazing cash flow generating machine fell in a heap without my father to run it. Losing my father's income was always going to create financial challenges, but selling the business for cents on the dollar made things even more difficult. It was only through the generosity of an old business partner that my mother managed to sell it for anything at all. My Dad was a great guy, and he loved us very much, but his optimism and comfort with risk meant that there was very little insurance in place to cushion the blow of losing the household's primary income and the value of what he would have thought was the primary asset (the business) in the household.

If you sell general insurance solutions, this is something you need to understand about the people whose businesses you protect with the insurance you sell. If you genuinely care about these people, you need to look beyond the business and understand that they have personal lives, families and dreams that simply won't be achieved if a personal insurance event occurs.

If you see your role as selling or account managing business customers as a job it's highly likely you can't tell me anything about your client's personal insurance situation. If you see selling insurance as more than a job and wish you did know, there's a high probability nobody has ever taught you how to engage a business owner in relation to this aspect of their personal life.

In this chapter I'm going to do that. I'll take you through several business risks you may not have thought about. These types of risks may not be the risks you insure, but they exist in nearly all businesses. And when something happens to a business owner, those are the risks that turn what the family (and you) thought was an amazing asset, into a major problem for the surviving family.

PROVOKING THE PROBLEM IS ALL YOU NEED TO DO

I'm not suggesting that general insurance salespeople (or accountants or lawyers) need to become experts in having detailed discussions with their business customers.

All you need to do is open up a conversation about the problems that a business owner may not be acknowledging. Once you've opened that conversation and helped the business owner acknowledge the problem, suggesting they meet with a specialist in that personal area is easy.

I'll give you some examples of how to weave a discussion on these risks into the conversation. Your primary outcome is to identify whether the risk is relevant. If it is, turn that into a reason for meeting with someone from the team who can help them cover the risk that their business might not be the asset they think it is, if something happens to them. Over time, I want you to build the confidence to be more direct and confident in promoting a review of personal insurances. But as a starting point, the following will provide you with strategies for making these conversations a part of your natural customer conversations.

RISK #1

LACK OF COVER IN SUPERANNUATION/ GROUP COVER

Let's assume that the business owner does have this type of insurance in place. In my experience, where there is a family home with a mortgage and a family, there is not enough cover provided by these sorts of policies to achieve what a business owner would want for their family if something happened to them.

For most business owners, this an even bigger problem because the default level of cover is often driven by the level of wages. And what do most business owners do?

Pay themselves lower wages than they should be paid!

Here's a more detailed example of how you might highlight this sort of issue:

SALESPERSON *"Roger, how do you figure out how much to pay yourself in wages?"*

ROGER "Basically what's available once everyone else gets paid."

SALESPERSON *"That's a common answer. Do you pay yourself market rate for the hours you work and all the work you do?"*

ROGER "Probably not."

SALESPERSON *"That's common, too. How is that impacting your personal insurance cover?"*

ROGER "What do you mean?"

SALESPERSON *"If you're paying yourself below market, it means that any insurance you have in your super is likely to be lower than it should be, given the work you do. Do you know how much insurance there is in your super policy?"*

ROGER "Not really."

SALESPERSON. *"That's OK. It's rare that any of our business owners, or even their employees, can answer that with any certainty. I'm keen to get one of the personal team to talk to you about that and make sure you know the answer. Can I set that up for you over the next few weeks?"*

Other examples of questions you might use to engage in a discussion around this include:

- *How did you choose a super (group cover in the USA) fund for all your employees?*

- *What's the insurance like in the default super fund you chose for your employees?*

- *Do you pay your super into the same fund as your employees?*

RISK #2

OVER-RELIANCE ON THE BUSINESS OWNER

Think about a customer you really enjoy working with and the owner of that business. Take a little time out to think about the day-to-day life of the business owner and all the things they do in the business. Now imagine they're gone. They can't be reached on the phone. They had no time to do a handover, and the business needs to open its doors and trade solvently.

How do you think the business would run? How many people would they have to hire to do all the work of the owner?

The simple reality is that for most businesses, the impact would be very significant – if not fatal to the business. Most businesses simply don't function without the business owner, and that's why most business owners don't take many six-week vacations. If the business owners you insure are too busy to talk to you, too busy to consider new types of cover and too busy to fill out details for underwriting applications, there's a high probability their business is overly reliant on them staying alive and in the business.

When you hear how busy a business owner is, this needs to be a trigger to engage them to ensure they've thought through insuring that risk.

Here's an example of a strategy for engaging in this type of discussion.

SALESPERSON *"Great to hear things are busy, Jenny.* **What's taking most of your time?"**

> JENNY "I'm flat out with a few new clients, and there's a lot they want delivered in the next few weeks. Can we put off the paperwork until I get through this backlog of work?"

SALESPERSON *"Not really, Jenny. Your insurance expires in about 14 days, so if we put it off, you'll be uninsured. I'll help you with the application so we can save you some time and get it done, but it needs to be done as fast as possible, so I can get it to the underwriter for approval in the next 48 hours to make sure we meet the expiry deadline. Can we just get it done now?"*

JENNY "OK. What do you need to know?"

SALESPERSON *"I'm just pulling up the forms now so we can get it done.* **Is there anyone else who can help you with all the work you've got on?"**

JENNY "Not really. It's all design work, and I promised the client I would do the work as part of getting the business."

SALESPERSON *"Understand, Jenny. The form's coming up now, and we can get started. Something I'm keen to do is get Jim from our personal insurance team to talk to you in a few weeks when things calm down a little. He takes care of the personal stuff for our business owners,* **and if there's work in the business only you can do and relationships only you can manage, I'm keen for you to consider how much key person risk there is in the business.** *Can I set that up for you when I get back the office?"*

Other examples of questions you might use to engage in a discussion around this include:

- *Who does all your work when you're on holidays?*

- *How effectively does the business run if you take an extended holiday?*

- *Is there anyone in the business who can do everything you do?*

RISK #3

OVER-RELIANCE ON THE OWNER'S PERSONAL RELATIONSHIPS

When a business loses a great salesperson, it's a tough day in the office. Obviously, there's the loss of someone the owner probably had a lot of history with, but there's also the high probability that the salesperson will take many relationships with them to their new employer or business. This may not happen immediately, but if the salesperson is good, it will happen over time.

Relationships with owners tend to be even deeper. So, when something happens to a business owner, and they're no longer in the business, the impact can be catastrophic. But, as with other risks like this, most business owners are very good at deleting or remaining in their existing state of denial. An example of how you might heighten an owner's awareness and acknowledgement of this type of risk is as follows:

SALESPERSON *"Bill, something I've been talking about to a few other business owners, is **how long they would have to work in the business if they sold it to another person.** One owner was telling me he was offered a great purchase price, but had to work in the business for three years before he got all the money. **What sort of handcuffs** do you think a purchaser would put on you if you sold the business?"*

BILL "Probably a year or two."

SALESPERSON *"Why so long?"*

BILL "There is lots to learn and lots of relationships to hand over. So, they would want to make sure they had control of those before they let me go."

SALESPERSON *"How much insurance do you have in place **to cover off that risk?"***

Other examples of questions you might use to engage in a discussion around this include:

- *Do you do a lot of the relationship management with your more important customers?*

- *How important are your personal relationships with customers?*

- *If you sold the business, would that have an impact on how many of your existing customers stayed?*

RISK #4

BUSINESS DEBT OVERFLOW INTO PERSONAL ASSETS

When you start a business, it's amazing how a desperation for cash flow causes you to use every available source of funding available. We all love the stories about successful entrepreneurs who were down to their last dollar or using credit cards to fund wages when they were growing the business. As a business grows and evolves, funding generally moves to using bank finance, but this comes with things like personal guarantees and debt secured by personal assets like the family home. And as a business owner who's been through all the challenges – it is amazing when you look back and consider how many times you nearly lost the house! When you're alive and well, you can manage all that risk by working hard and running a great business and, over time, you get very good at convincing yourself it's not really a risk at all. The problem is that if you die or can't work, you have no ability to manage that risk and as the business hurts, the risk of the bank asking for its money back and leveraging guarantees and security increases significantly.

I personally don't think chasing money that's owed by a business owner from personal assets is evil or inappropriate. Banks put in place safeguards for the risks they take on business owners by gaining guarantees and security over the assets the business owner has available. If a business owner wants to take risks with a bank's money, they need to understand that they're taking risk with the security they've provided. But let's not get caught up in this, because we know that if the business owner had the right personal insurance in place this risk could have been managed.

Here's an example of how you might bring this sort of risk to the attention of a business owner and encourage them to discuss it with one of your specialists in this area:

SALESPERSON *"You've experienced a lot of growth this year. How have you found funding all the expansion?"*

MARY "It's been tough, but we seem to be making it all happen. We got some funding from the bank, and we've had to improve our collection of money owing."

SALESPERSON *"Great. And how are you managing the risk on your personal assets in relation to the extra funding?"*

MARY "What do you mean?"

SALESPERSON *"If you've got guarantees in place or there's security over the home, then more growth means more exposure for personal assets if something happens to you or someone else who's important in the business. Have you reviewed the policies on that type of stuff?"*

MARY "Not really."

SALESPERSON *"That's OK. Most of my customers who are busy with growth are too busy to think about this sort of cover. I'll get Judy from our personal team to drop in and have a chat with you about it all. Is next week OK?"*

Other examples of questions you might use to engage in a discussion around this include:

- *With all the growth you're going through, have you had time to think about how that could impact your personal assets like the home?*

- *Have you had time to review all your personal insurance considering how much the business and your revenue have grown over the past three years?*

- *Have you done any scenario planning on how exposed your personal assets are to what goes on in the business?*

RISK #5

UNINTENDED PARTNERSHIPS

I love my business partner dearly. We have similar values, very different skills and what he brings to the table is something I could never have delivered to the business we've built. I'm also very fond of his wife, who is an intelligent, caring and loving partner. But I wouldn't want to be in business with his wife because she doesn't bring to the table what he does or what the business needs.

"Where is this going?"

you may be asking. Well, if he dies and we don't have the right cover in place, she gets his shares in the business and becomes my business partner. This is a lot more common than you think. And, life has been very good to me, but I would struggle to find the cash required to buy those shares from her. Even if could fund this, it would be financially challenging and mean I'm borrowing money against a business that has just lost a founding partner critical to the business.

This is something that can and should be avoided, with the right legal agreements and personal cover to fund the acquisition of the deceased partner's shares. This discussion is probably the easiest to engage a business owner in and it goes something like this.

SALESPERSON *"Can I ask you both a personal question?"*

BILL/MARY "Sure."

SALESPERSON *"Is there a reason the two of you are in partnership and didn't include each other's spouses in the business when you founded it?"*

MARY "Well, my husband came after we founded the business and he has a great job anyway. And Bill's wife is flat out with her business and the family."

SALESPERSON *"OK. Have you discussed what would happen if something did happen to either of you and the other person's spouse gained control of their shares?"*

Other examples of questions you might use to engage in a discussion around this include:

- *Have you ever talked through what happens if something happens to either partner and that partner can no longer work in the business?*

- *Do you have an option agreement in place to cover each other if something happens to one of you?*

- *Have you valued up the shares in the business to agree on a purchase price if something happens to one of you?*

Generally, this is an easy conversation. People will often tell you they've put this in place, but from personal experience I can tell you two things: first, when a professional reviews the structure of the agreements and insurance, there is almost always a way to improve things – and generally several mistakes. Second, if the business has grown, the insurance that was taken out in the early stages of the business is no longer enough to fund a fair purchase price for the shares.

RISK #6

INAPPROPRIATE COVER

Structuring the right personal insurance can be incredibly complex for a business owner. This is even more the case when they are exposed to other structures like partnerships and shareholder agreements.

Cover can be inappropriate for several reasons. The business may have grown significantly, and the insurance they put in place three to five years ago may no longer match their current lifestyle; they may have exposed themselves to significant debt in the business and not adjusted their personal insurance; they may have grown the family and been too busy in the business to adjust the insurance in their personal life. The way they make payments may be inefficient from a tax perspective, either through poor structuring or changes to the law, and they may have just got bad initial advice, which unfortunately is so often the case.

Questions you might ask to provoke this problem include:

- *A lot has changed in the business over the past five years. Has your personal insurance kept up?*

- *With all the debt you've taken on to fund growth over the last few years, have you considered how that should be reflected in your personal insurance?*

- *OK, so X is your accountant, and I'll note that on the application. Where do you get all your personal insurance advice from? Why them?*

RISK #7

CASH FLOW RISK IN THE BUSINESS

Most business owners generally get excited when sales are great, but smart business owners also get concerned. There are two reasons for concern. Generally, to deliver on the increased sales, you need to outlay significant money to fulfil sales demand. The first concern you should have is "can I fund the goods or services to deliver on what we've sold?" But there's another even bigger concern, which is around payment for those goods or services. Many of the businesses you insure send an invoice and await payment, and that can take 30 to 90 days – or even longer on big contracts. These two things create a cash flow gap between the time a business owner pays for goods or services and the time their customers pay.

Often, the faster you grow, the bigger the gap – and generally the tougher the market, the more eager you are to sell and the harder it is to collect payment. So, despite looking like a fantastic business on paper, many of the businesses you think are great are often struggling for cash, because it's all locked up with debtors who have not yet paid for the goods and services they've consumed.

When something happens to a business owner that takes them out of the business, three things almost always happen, and a fourth often happens. First, fewer sales are made because the owner is not making sales. Second, fewer sales are made because the staff are dealing with the loss of the owner and struggling without them in the business. Third, people who are owed money generally want to get paid as soon as possible, because the person they trust to pay them is no longer alive or in control. And fourth, which is sad, people who owe money often delay payment because the owner isn't chasing it. When these four things happen, even the best business can become insolvent and incredibly difficult to sell. The value of the business asset can deteriorate at an incredibly fast rate.

I'm not recommending that you get into a detailed conversation with the customer about cash flow unless you're confident and comfortable with that sort of conversation. The point here is that most businesses are not a good insurance policy.

COMMIT TO PROTECTING OWNERS BEYOND THE BUSINESS

As I mentioned before, if you truly care about the relationships you have with your customers, you need to go beyond the products you sell and understand the risks a business creates in people's personal lives. Failing to engage in this discussion is failing to truly protect and provide. Failing to understand the risk your customers are exposed to because it's slightly inconvenient or uncomfortable to include in the conversation is not customer centric.

I challenge all of you in this space to make this a part of your conversations.

About
The Author

Dean Mannix is the CEO and a co-founder of SalesITV, SalesROI and Cadence.coach.

He has delivered sales performance projects in over 25 countries and is recognised as one of Australia's leading sales performance authorities. Over the past two decades, Dean has worked globally with a diverse range of clients including Goldman Sachs, Westpac, Oracle, Canon, News Corp, Commbank, Macquarie Bank, Nomura Securities, Fairfax, Deutsche Bank, BT Financial Group, NAB, Suncorp, Bank of Queensland and the Boston Consulting Group.

Dean draws on personal experience developed across a diverse range of industries, with 30 years of legal, finance, sales, management and consulting experience. He completed his General Registered Representative qualifications with the London Stock Exchange while working with Morgan Stanley in London. Dean then went on to complete his Law Degree and was admitted as a Solicitor practising in litigation and negotiating complex disputes for some of Australia's largest construction companies. His next role, as CEO, was leading a property development and childcare management company to build and manage a team of 140 employees. This business was successfully developed and sold. He then developed and led a highly successful sales team in the technology space and simultaneously grew his consulting business before focusing solely on sales performance.

For the past decade Dean has authored and presented over 150 video training programs now available through SalesITV (enterprise customers) and SalesROI (small business and individual customers).

Dean holds a Law Degree from QUT, an Executive MBA from the AGSM and he is also a qualified Yoga teacher.

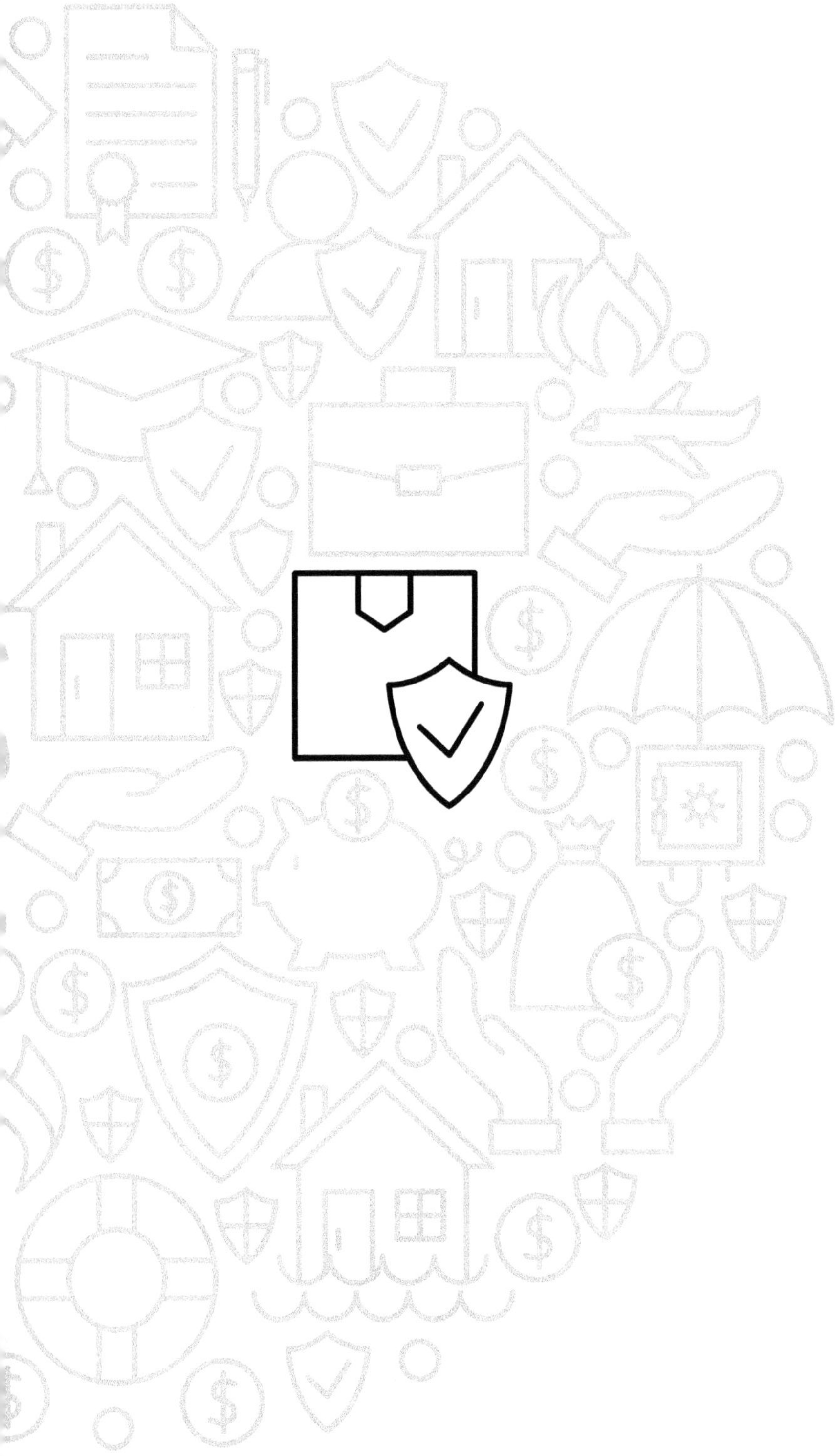

APPENDIX

THE PROTECT AND PROVIDE CODE

I am an insurance professional committed to protecting, providing and producing every day to ensure the success and wellbeing of my customers, the insurer(s) I sell insurance for, myself and those I love.

What I do matters. I am absolutely committed to protecting:

- *Every person I engage from the pain they and their families will face in the event of an unexpected uninsured event.*

- *Every person I engage in the insurance conversation from the biases that make them delete, diminish and deny the need to insure.*

- *My employer's/provider's brand and the trust that brand creates in the insured's mind.*

- *My ability to work in the industry and my personal reputation.*

When people claim on the insurance I sell it makes a profound difference in their lives and the lives of those they love. I am committed to:

- *Ensuring every person I have the insurance conversation with is able to provide for themselves and their families if an insurance event occurs.*

- *Ensuring my employer/provider can continue to provide me with the solutions and environment required for my success and the wellbeing of my customers.*

- *Ensuring my efforts translate to the ability to provide the quality of life deserved for my commitment and contribution, including my family's sacrifices and support.*

CITATIONS

Chapter 2

1. Thomas, A. K.; Millar, P. R. (2011). "Reducing the Framing Effect in Older and Younger Adults by Encouraging Analytic Processing". The Journals of Gerontology Series B: Psychological Sciences and Social Sciences. 67B (2): 139.

2. Gächter, S.; Orzen, H.; Renner, E.; Stamer, C. (2009). "Are experimental economists prone to framing effects? A natural field experiment". Journal of Economic Behavior & Organization.

3. Gonzales M.H., Aronson E., Costanzo M.A., (1988). "Using Social Cognition and Persuasion to Promote Energy Conservation: A Quasi-Experiment". Journal of Applied Social Psychology.

4. Kahneman, D. & Tversky, A. (1984). "Choices, Values, and Frames". American Psychologist. 39 (4): 341–350.

5. Kahneman, D. & Tversky, A. (1992). "Advances in prospect theory: Cumulative representation of uncertainty". Journal of Risk and Uncertainty. 5 (4): 297–323

6. 2016 American Household Credit Card Debt Study https://www.nerdwallet.com/blog/average-credit-card-debt-household/

7. Australian Credit Card and Debit Card Statistics 2017 https://www.finder.com.au/credit-cards/credit-card-statistics

Chapter 5

8. Influence, The Psychology of Persuasion. Cialdini. 1984 Harper Press page 85

Chapter 9

9. I hope this doesn't damage my credibility with you, but unfortunately, I've been unable to locate the citation for this research.

10. Covey, S. R. (2004). The 7 habits of highly effective people: Restoring the character ethic. New York: Free Press.

11. Sinek, S. (2011). Start with why: How great leaders inspire everyone to take action. Portfolio/Penguin.

Chapter 10

12. Scott, S. (2002). Fierce conversations: Achieving success at work & in life, one conversation at a time. New York, N.Y.: Viking.

13. Maister, D. H., Green, C. H., & Galford, R. M. (2000). The trusted advisor. New York: Free Press.

Chapter 14

14. Seligman, M. E. P. (2006). Learned optimism: How to change your mind and your life. New York: Vintage Books.

www.ingramcontent.com/pod-product-compliance
Lightning Source LLC
Chambersburg PA
CBHW060323200326

41519CB00011BA/1818